Secret Records Revealed

I know of the operations of this network [of power] . . . and was permitted for two years, in the early 1960s, to examine its papers and secret records. I have no aversion to it. . . .

—*Prof. Carroll Quigley* (Bill Clinton's mentor at Georgetown University)

▪▪▪▪▪

Norman Cousins worked for world peace and world government. . . . Best wishes for an enjoyable reception and for future success.

—*President William Clinton,* June 22, 1993, in a letter on White House stationery to the World Federalist Association on the occasion of its Global Governance Award honoring its past president, Norman Cousins.

SECRET RECORDS REVEALED

Printed in the United States of America

Published by
Hearthstone Publishing, Ltd.
500 Beacon Dr. ▪ Oklahoma City, OK 73127
405/789-3885 ▪ 800/652-1144 ▪ FAX 405/789-6502

Cover design by Christi Killian
ISBN 1-57558-031-4

Secret Records Revealed

The Men, the Money, and the Methods Behind the New World Order

DENNIS LAURENCE CUDDY, Ph.D.

The Bank for International Settlements

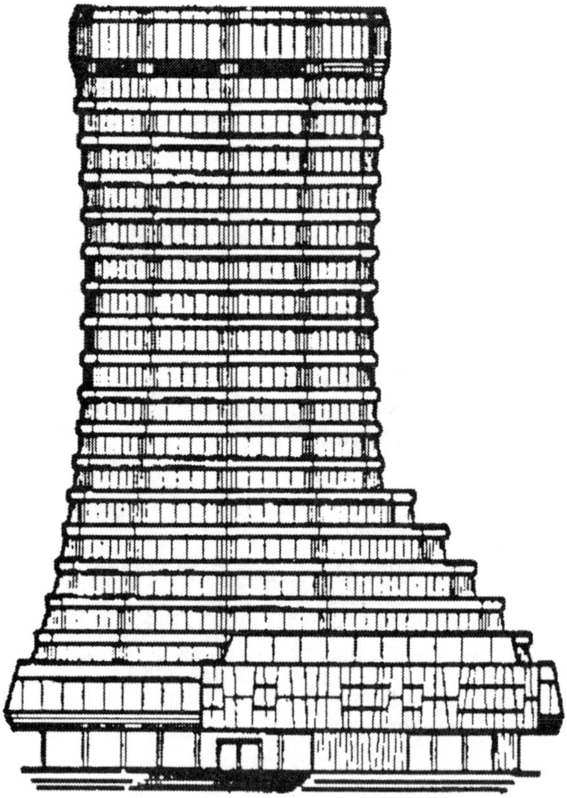

In George Orwell's *1984*, a description of the future under "Big Brother" is given as "a boot stamping on a human face — forever." Could the "boot" be the new eighteen-story Bank for International Settlements (BIS) which was completed in Basel, Switzerland, in 1977 in the shape of a boot (see picture above), and became known as the "Tower of Basel"? The BIS was originally founded by J. P. Morgan and Co. and others under the Hague Agreement of 1930 as *the* bank for central banks (e.g., U.S. Federal Reserve, German Bundesbank, Bank of Japan, etc.) around the world and exempt from taxation.

On August 5, 1995, *The New York Times* published an article by Keith Bradsher, in which he wrote:

> In a small Swiss city sits an international organization so obscure and secretive. . . . Control of the institution, the Bank for International Settlements, lies with some of the world's most powerful and least visible men: the heads of thirty-two central banks, officials able to shift billions of dollars and alter the course of economies at the stroke of a pen.

On June 28, 1998, *The Washington Post* published an article about the Bank for International Settlements (BIS) titled, "At Secret Meetings in Switzerland, 13 People Shape the World's Economy," which described these individuals as "this economic cabal . . . this secretive group . . . the financial barons who control the world's supply of money."

After financial consultant Joan Veon attended the business meeting of the Bank for International Settlements in June 1998, she wrote in her newsletter that

> . . . the Bank for International Settlements designed the present borderless flow of monies between countries when it pushed for the deregulation (1980) of monetary laws of the major North American, European, and Asian countries. By tearing down national financial borders, they created the ability for $1.2 trillion daily to flow around the world (uncontrolled stateless money) looking for the highest interest or fastest currency play.

On ABC's television's "Nightline" (July 1, 1998), David Turecamo stated concerning certain international investors, that they can "topple politicians with the click of a mouse . . . who can move huge amounts of money into and out of markets in a nanosecond. . . . Money knows no allegiance. There is no patriotism." Host Ted Koppel's response to that was, "Wouldn't you know it, when we're the last remaining superpower, it doesn't count anymore. Is that what you're saying?" And Turecamo replied: "That's it. That's exactly it."

Dedicated to the memory of
my father
JOSEPH LEO CUDDY

whose life was in selfless service to God, to his family, and to his country and its constitutional principles. With many other brave Americans, he fought in the Second World War to defend freedom. He was awarded a number of medals, including the Legion of Merit and the Bronze Star, while serving in the 633rd Field Artillery, which was in combat for a record number of consecutive days. Of historic note, "A" Battery of the 633rd Field Artillery was organized and equipped by Alexander Hamilton in 1776. My father was always an inspiration to many in his dedication to duty, a ready smile and a sense of humor, and the cheerfulness he maintained even through long years of suffering.

Introduction

In the mid-1960s, when Bill Clinton was a student at Georgetown University, his mentor there was Prof. Carroll Quigley, who authored *Tragedy and Hope* in 1966. Twenty-six years later, then-Governor Clinton would be elected President of the United States, and James K. Fitzpatrick would write on the editorial page of the national newspaper *The Wanderer,* November 18, 1993, A.D.:

> Clinton told reporters in an interview that Quigley's work centered on the existence of a permanent shadow government of powerful bankers and businessmen and government officials that controls the agenda of our political life from behind the scenes. Clinton spoke in that interview of coming to the conclusion, while still a young man, that it was necessary for him to gain access to the inner circle of this group in order to become part of the decision-making process that shapes our world.

This "inner circle" is perhaps connected historically to the "Circle of Initiates," who were part of Cecil Rhodes' plan for world domination. Rhodes biographer Sarah

Millin wrote: "The government of the world was Rhodes' simple desire." To control "the government of the world," of course, would take a considerable amount of money. And regarding the source of Rhodes' funds, Prof. Quigley wrote in *Tragedy and Hope:*

> With financial support from Lord Rothschild and Alfred Beit, he [Rhodes] was able to monopolize the diamond mines of South Africa as De Beers Consolidated Mines and to build up a great gold mining enterprise as Consolidated Gold Fields.

Rhodes had been inspired by John Ruskin (who has a swastiska on his grave), who in turn had been influenced by commune organizer Robert Owen. These men were elitist socialists, with Ruskin writing: "There is a destiny now possible to us—the highest ever set before a nation to be accepted or refused. We are still undegenerate in race; a race mingled of the best northern blood."

In *Time and Tide* (1867), Ruskin wrote that

> the first duty of a State is to see that every child born therein shall be well housed, clothed, fed and educated. . . . But in order to the effecting this the Government must have an authority over the people of which we now do not so much as dream.

His views were based to some extent on those of socialist Robert Owen, who began the first commune in America in 1825 at New Harmony, Indiana, stating:

> I am come to this country to introduce an entire new order of society; to change it from the ignorant selfish system, to an enlightened social system, which shall gradually unite all interests into one and remove all cause for contest between individuals.

Ruskin read Plato every day (e.g., Plato's *Republic,* a "Republic of Philosophers") and believed in government by the elite who would control means of production and distribution. This was similar to the socialist concept of the French Revolution, in which "philosopher-kings" would exercise rule over the masses.

In Cecil Rhodes' "Confession of Faith" (1875), written shortly before the time of his first will in 1877, he expressed an elitist view similar to that stated by John Ruskin concerning "the best northern blood," when Rhodes remarked: "I contend that we are the finest race in the world and that the more of the world we inhabit the better it is for the human race."

Rhodes' plan for world domination included, according to his "Confession of Faith," the foundation of "so great a power as to hereafter render wars impossible." It involved establishing a secret society [headed by Sir Alfred (Lord) Milner after Rhodes' death and hereafter referred to as "The Group"], and the Rhodes Scholarships (RS), one of which would be held by Bill Clinton. The scholarships were to attend Oxford University, where the winter term (January to March) was called "Hilary." According to Prof. Quigley in *The Anglo-American Establishment* (written 1949, published 1981):

> The [Rhodes] scholarships were merely a facade to

> conceal the secret society, or, more accurately, they were to be one of the instruments by which members of the secret society could carry out Rhodes' purpose.

And the reason Quigley's revelations are so credible is that he stated in *Tragedy and Hope* that he had been allowed to examine the "secret records" of this network of power for a couple of years and was largely sympathetic to their aims.[1]

The Group's basic objective was to penetrate and control the areas of politics, economics, education, and journalism. And a key criterion for anyone being accepted for participation in their plan was that the individual (e.g., Rhodes Scholar) must believe that the first duty of any man is to serve society and the State.

The way the idea would work would be that after three or four decades, enough individuals would be in positions of influence so that a conspiracy would no longer be necessary. Rather, these individuals with a one-world elitist outlook would simply open doors to positions of prominence for other like-minded globalists, who in turn would do likewise for others. It would operate like the old political adage that "personnel is policy."

In *Cowboys Into Gentlemen: Rhodes Scholars, Oxford, and the Creation of an American Elite* (1998), authors Thomas and Kathleen Schaeper write:

> [Frank] Aydelotte (American Secretary to the Rhodes Trustees) also became known as a sort of "kingmaker" of college presidents. He believed that the best way

to promote academic excellence was to appoint Rhodes Scholars to every vacancy for college presidencies or deanships. Whenever he heard that a university was seeking a new executive or dean, he worked his private networks to ensure that Rhodes Scholars received serious consideration. Though no selection committee would ever admit it, it was widely believed that dozens of college presidents and deans owed their new jobs to his cloakroom lobbying. . . . In the world of business, Rhodes Scholars have occupied virtually every level of every field. . . . Nearly every field in the world of business has, at one time or another, had a Rhodes Scholar at or near its pinnacle. . . . The huge investment banking firm of Goldman Sachs has included dozens of [Rhodes] scholars over the past half century, but never as many as in the 1990s, when at any given moment at least a half dozen have been partners. . . . Many [Rhodes] scholars agree that there is one area in which a strong Oxford network does seem to operate: government. . . . Many [Rhodes] scholars must have winced when they read the [London] *Sunday Telegraph*'s [March 21] 1993 article on Stan McGee [Rhodes Scholar 1992]. The newspaper's reporter . . . noted that . . . above McGee's bed was a world map with thumb tacks stuck into those places he had "conquered." McGee said that a Rhodes Scholarship was important as "an entree into the power elite."

The following chronology will demonstrate how Rhodes' plan for an elitist-controlled socialist "New World Order" developed over the years, along with quotations and activities of Rhodes Scholars (RS) who have played an important part in furthering Rhodes' elitist goals.

Chronology

1890

▪ Autumn: Rhodes sends a letter to his close friend W. T. Stead regarding his plan:

> The key of my idea discussed with you is a Society, copied from the Jesuits as to organization . . . an idea which ultimately (leads) to the cessation of all wars and one language throughout the world. . . . The only thing feasible to carry this idea out is a secret one [society] gradually absorbing the wealth of the world to be devoted to such an object. . . . Fancy the charm to young America . . . to share in a scheme to take the government of the whole world!

Rhodes' "universal peace" would begin, according to him, "after one hundred years," and it will be exactly one hundred years later in the autumn of 1990 that President George Bush will spell out his "New World Order" concept for universal peace and cooperation. The contents of Rhodes' letter will be published in W. T. Stead's article in *Review of Reviews* (May 1902), and regarding the Rhodes Scholars and Rhodes' plan stated in 1890, Prof. Quigley would later write:

> . . . after thirty years there would be "between two and three thousand men in the prime of life scattered all over the world, each one of whom, moreover, would have been specially—mathematically—selected toward the Founder's purposes" (Quigley quoting Stead).

And according to Rhodes biographer Sarah Millin, Rhodes told Stead that the scholars should have the following characteristics: "smugness, brutality, unctuous rectitude, and tact." In the future, President Clinton will be described as smug and brutal. Also, concerning "unctuous rectitude," *Webster's Dictionary* defines "unctuous" as "oily in speech or manner; plastic; moldable; characterized by a smug, smooth pretense of spiritual feeling, fervor, or earnestness, as in seeking to persuade." This will fit the nickname "Slick Willie" given to Bill Clinton.

1891

- February 5: Rhodes' secret society, "The Society of the Elect," is formally established (with the central part established by March). Rhodes is the "General," with Stead, Milner, and Reginald Baliol Brett (Lord Esher) forming the executive committee. They were followed by the "Circle of Initiates," with an "Association of Helpers" (later organized by Milner as the semi-secret Round Table Groups) beyond them.

1895

- The Fabian Socialists establish the London School of Economics. Though the Fabians are dominated by an intellectual elite, and The Group is dominated by a financial elite, they both believe in a socialist relationship between government and the masses of people, who should be led and cared for by an elitist-controlled government.[2] Though the Fabians and The Group have differences of opinion which are significant, The Group will come to greatly influence the London School of Economics, which will later have a Center for the Study of Global Governance.

H. G. Wells, the noted Fabian, will write books such as *The Open Conspiracy: Blue Prints for a World Revolution* (1928) and *The New World Order* (1939), outlining the coming World Socialist Government. And in Wells' *New Worlds for Old* (1908), he will describe how socialism could be achieved without public support through a slowly executed "plot," training people (e.g., in the London School of Economics) and placing them in the government bureaucracy where they will remain indefinitely (while elected political leaders come and go) developing and enforcing socialistic rules and regulations.

1898

▪ Rhodes in a conversation with Stead (friend of renowned occultist Annie Besant) says, "I support Milner absolutely without reserve. Whatever happens, I say ditto to Milner." This is similar to what President Woodrow Wilson would say about Col. Edward Mandell House: "Mr. House is my second personality. . . . His thoughts and mine are one." House in 1912 will author *Philip Dru: Administrator* promoting "socialism as dreamed of by Karl Marx." And in 1918 President Wilson's Secretary of the

Interior, Franklin Lane, will write to a personal friend concerning House's book: "All that book has said should be, comes about. The president comes to Philip Dru in the end."

1901

- *Social Control* by Edward Alsworth Ross is published. Ross is known as the "Father of American Sociology," and in this book, he reveals that social checks and stimuli "are managed by a rather small knot of persons . . . the Elite. . . . Judgment may be moulded as well as the will and the feelings."

1902

- *The Last Will and Testament of Cecil Rhodes* by W. T. Stead is published, in which Stead describes Rhodes' plan as "a vision." Bill Clinton (Rhodes Scholar 1968) in the 1992 presidential race will have as his campaign theme that he has "a vision."

- *Our Benevolent Feudalism* by W. J. Ghent (former editor of the *American Fabian*) is published (see p. 221). It will be referred to in Jack London's *The Iron Heal* (1907) as "the textbook" the "oligarchs" will use to rule in the future. London will say they (and the plutocrats) will have new ways "of moulding the thought processes of the nation," and that the banks will constitute

> one of the most important forces of the Oligarchy. . . . The labor castes, the Mercenaries, and the great hordes of secret agents and police . . . were all pledged to the

> Oligarchy. . . . The condition of the people of the abyss was pitiable. . . . All their old liberties were gone. They were labor-slaves. Choice of work was denied them. Likewise was denied them . . . the right to bear or possess arms. They were not land-serfs like the farmers. They were machine-serfs and labor-serfs.

1902–1910

▪ Various branches of the Carnegie Trust (e.g., Carnegie Foundation, Carnegie Endowment for International Peace, etc.) are established.[3] The Group is very close to banker J. P. Morgan, who has a strong influence on branches of the Carnegie Trust. Andrew Carnegie has been very sympathetic to Rhodes' plan.[4]

In 1902 Daniel Coit Gilman becomes the first president of the Carnegie Institution of Washington, D.C. He is a member of the "Skull and Bones" society (into which George Bush, David Boren, etc., will be initiated), and in 1898 invited Fabian Socialists Beatrice and Sidney Webb to address the faculty of Johns Hopkins University where he was president. There, he had hired G. Stanley Hall, who became the mentor of John Dewey ("Father of Progressive Education," a founder of the Intercollegiate Socialist Society, and co-author of the first *Humanist Manifesto* in 1933).

In 1904, the Carnegie Institution, with Gilman as president, finances the establishment of a biological experiment station related to eugenics at Cold Spring Harbor, New York. Charles Davenport is the director. On today's (1999) Cold Spring Harbor Laboratory website (*http://www.cshl.org/public/history.htm*) one reads:

> By 1910 Davenport's interest had shifted to human genetics. In a classic example of well-intentioned but tragically misinformed science, Davenport established the Eugenics Record Office at Cold Spring Harbor, again with himself as director. Shut down in 1940, for over twenty years the ERO was the main setting for this dark chapter in the history of genetics.

In the late 1960s, Dr. James D. Watson will become director of Cold Spring Harbor Laboratory. And in the May 1973 edition of *Prism* (published by the American Medical Association) in an article titled "Children from the Laboratory," Dr. Watson will state:

> I think we must reevaluate our basic assumptions about the meaning of life. Perhaps . . . no one should be thought of as alive until about three days after birth. . . . If a child were not declared alive until three days after birth, then . . . the doctor could allow the child to die if the parents so chose.

In the 1990s, Dr. Watson will be president of Cold Spring Harbor Laboratory and will work on the Human Genome Project, to map out all the human genes, which he predicts will be completed by 2005.

In 1909, the Carnegie-published document, "Cecil Rhodes and His Scholars As Factors in International Conciliation," is released. It is written by the first Oxford Secretary to the Rhodes Trust, Francis Wylie, who suggests that to develop "so great a Power as to hereafter render wars impossible," a [secret] society be formed "to this end" and, "co-extensive with the British Empire, preaching imperial ideas, and *effecting its objectives through the control of education.*" He goes on to say that the objectives should be achieved in an "unobtrusive" manner, with influence "as subtle as it is leisurely."

1905

▪ Bernadotte Schmitt becomes a Rhodes Scholar, and he will later be president of the American Historical Association. (Also see first entry under 1920.)

▪ A. E. Rollins becomes a Rhodes Scholar, and he will later be managing editor of *Compton's Encyclopaedia.*

▪ Charles Mahaffie becomes a Rhodes Scholar, and in 1936 and 1949 he will be appointed chairman of the Interstate Commerce Commission.

1907

▪ Arthur Chenoweth becomes a Rhodes Scholar and will later be president of the Miss America Pageant.

▪ *Lord of the World* by Robert Hugh Benson is published, in which he writes:

> In 1917 . . . Communism really began. . . . The new order began then. . . . [After 1989] the final scheme of Western Free Trade. . . . Patriotism has been dying fast. . . . [There is] this European Parliament. . . . With the Release Act in 1998 . . . [there were] the ministers of euthanasia. . . . [The Lord of the World] had a mag-

> netic character . . . rising out of the heaving dun-coloured waters of American Socialism like a vision. . . . It will mean free trade all over the world. . . . Party must unite with party, country with country, and continent with continent. . . . America was powerless. . . . The appearance of peace deceived many. . . . The press was engineered with extraordinary adroitness. . . . The world is one now, not many. Individualism is dead. . . . The Humanity Religion was the only one. . . . Man was God. . . . No actual point of light breaking the appalling vault of gloom. . . .

See fuller quotation on pages 224–225 of *Secret Records Revealed.* It is remarkable that Benson in 1907 writes about communism really beginning in 1917, and the Russian Revolution will occur in 1917. It is remarkable that Benson in 1907 writes about "the final scheme of Western Free Trade after 1989," and the free trade agreements among leaders of the European Community will be reached in 1991, and President Bush will sign NAFTA in 1992. It is also remarkable that Benson in 1907 writes about "ministers of euthanasia in 1998," and many consider the activities of Jack Kevorkian in the U.S. and others in nations like Holland in the late 1990s to be like those of "ministers of euthanasia."

Robert Hugh Benson (born 1871) is the son of the Archbishop of Canterbury, Edward White Benson, who in 1883 married Mary Sidgwick. She is the sister of Prof. Henry Sidgwick (who would be Bertrand Russell's tutor), a founder of the Society for Psychical Research (SPR) along with future British prime minister Arthur Balfour (one of Cecil Rhodes' "Circle of Initiates"). John Ruskin, who inspired Cecil Rhodes, was an SPR member, as were Fabian Socialist founders Frank Podmore and Edward Pease. Another member of the SPR has been Prime Minister William Gladstone, who is a member of "The Cecil Bloc," identified by Prof. Carroll Quigley as the political influence behind Lord Alfred Milner's furtherance of Cecil Rhodes' plan for world dominion. Other members of "The Cecil Bloc" include Prime Minister Balfour, author Rudyard Kipling, and Lord Alfred Tennyson (SPR member) who had written "Locksley Hall" (1842), which called for "the parliament of man in the Federation of the world." President Harry Truman will carry this part of the poem with him in his pocket, explaining, "that's what I have been working for."

1910

▪ Edwin Hubble becomes a Rhodes Scholar. Even though he would use the racist words "darkies" and "pickaninnies" to refer to blacks, Oxford University will reward him with an honorary doctorate in 1934. He will help convince Albert Einstein in 1931 that a "big bang" occurred at the beginning of time, and NASA will name a space telescope after Hubble toward the end of the century.

▪ Robert Hale becomes a Rhodes Scholar. He will later become Speaker of the House of Representatives for the state of Maine, and then he will become a member of the U.S. House of Representatives.

1912

▪ J. P. Morgan and other leading bankers want establishment of the Federal Reserve, but it is opposed by President William Howard Taft, who looks like a sure winner over Democrat Woodrow Wilson. Morgan, however, finances the entry of Teddy Roosevelt into the race, thereby splitting the Republican ballots, allowing Wilson to win with only 42.5 percent of the popular vote. This is simi-

Robert Minor's cartoon depicting J. P. Morgan, Andrew Carnegie, John D. Rockefeller, Teddy Roosevelt, and other men of wealth, welcoming Karl Marx's socialism *(St. Louis Post-Dispatch,* 1911).

lar to the presidential race of 1992, when Ross Perot's entry will allow Bill Clinton to defeat President George Bush with only forty-three percent of the popular vote. Perot's political mentor will be Council on Foreign Relations (CFR) member Lloyd Cutler (a CFR director 1977–79), who will later become chief White House legal counsel to President Clinton to help him overcome the negative publicity concerning the "Whitewater" affair. Cutler will also want to change the U.S. Constitution's "separation of powers" and "checks and balances" provisions or characteristics in order to make our government more parliamentary.

▪ During the presidential campaign this year, Woodrow Wilson's national campaign vice-chairman, William McAdoo, proclaims the following:

> The fact is that there is a serious danger of this country becoming a pluto-democracy; that is, a sham republic with the real government in the hands of a small clique of enormously wealthy men, who speak through their money, and whose influence, even today, radiates to every corner of the United States.

President Wilson will appoint McAdoo as Secretary of the Treasury, and the above quote can be found in McAdoo's 1931 book, *Crowded Years.*

1913

▪ January: Joseph Stalin delivers an address in Vienna, in which he remarks:

> National autonomy does not solve the problem. . . . The only real solution is regional autonomy. . . . It does not divide people according to nation, it does not strengthen national partitions; on the contrary, it only serves to break down these partitions and unites the population in such a manner as to open the way for division of a different kind, division according to class.

Stalin is saying that national loyalties would become subservient to *regional* arrangements, which would facilitate Marx's "class struggle" with the eventual theme of "workers of the world unite" to establish the "dictatorship of the proletariat." This is similar to V. I. Lenin's "disunion for the purpose of union" theory, and in 1916 Lenin will proclaim: "The aim of socialism is not only to abolish the present division of mankind into smaller states and all-national isolation, not only to bring the nations closer to each other, but also to merge them."

▪ Prior to the passage of the Federal Reserve Act, President Wilson's *The New Freedom* is published, in which he reveals:

> Since I entered politics, I have chiefly had men's views confided to me privately. Some of the biggest men in the U.S., in the field of commerce and manufacturing, are afraid of somebody, are afraid of something. They know that there is a power somewhere so organized, so subtle, so watchful, so interlocked, so complete, so pervasive, that they had better not speak above their breath when they speak in condemnation of it. . . . We have been dreading all along the time when the com-

> bined power of high finance would be greater than the power of government. . . . We have come to be one of the worst ruled, one of the most completely controlled and dominated, governments in the civilized world—no longer a government by free opinion, no longer a government by conviction and the vote of the majority, but a government by the opinion and duress of small groups of dominant men. . . . We are in a new world. . . . I speak of the control over the government exercised by Big Business. Behind the whole subject, of course, is the truth that, in the new order, government and business must be associated closely. . . . We stand in the presence of a revolution . . . (which) will come in peaceful guise. . . . Some radical changes we must make in our law and practice. Some reconstructions . . . which a new age and new circumstances impose upon us.

These remarks came from his campaign speeches late in 1912.

▪ December 23: President Wilson signs the Federal Reserve Act. One of the individuals who helped to plan the Federal Reserve is Frank Vanderlip, president of Rockefeller's National City Bank, who will write in *The Saturday Evening Post* (February 9, 1935) that he "was as secretive—indeed as furtive—as any conspirator" in the execution of their plans to form that body.

▪ O. C. Carmichael becomes a Rhodes Scholar, and will be chancellor of Vanderbilt University, chairman of the

Board of Trustees of the State University of New York, president of the University of Alabama, and president of the Carnegie Foundation for the Advancement of Teaching 1946–1953. He's a lifetime member of the National Education Association.

▪ Brand Blanshard becomes a Rhodes Scholar and will later sign *The Humanist Manifesto* (as will his twin brother, Paul). He will win a "Humanist Pioneer" award and be on the editorial advisory board of *The Humanist* magazine.

▪ The (Rockefeller) General Education Board publishes "The Country School of To-Morrow" by board chairman Frederick Gates, who declares:

> In our dream, we have limitless resources, and the people yield themselves with perfect docility to our molding hand. The present educational conventions fade from our minds; and, unhampered by tradition, we work our own good will upon a grateful and responsive rural folk. We shall not try to make these people or any of their children into philosophers or men of learning or science. We are not to raise up from among them authors, orators, poets, or men of letters. We shall not search for embryo great artists, painters, musicians. . . .

1914

▪ May 29: Many weeks *before* the assassination of Archduke Franz Ferdinand (on June 28), which will serve as the catalyst for the beginning of World War I, Col. House in Berlin writes to President Wilson: "Whenever England consents, France and Russia will close in on Germany and Austria." Then, on July 20 and 29, British Secretary of State Sir Edward Grey ("close to the Milner Group politically, intellectually, and socially," according to Prof. Quigley) will make certain statements to the German Ambassador to England (Prince Karl Max Lichnowsky) that do not make it clear Britain will enter the conflict (World War I) if Germany goes to war. Had a clear message been sent, it is possible the First World War could have been avoided.

This sounds similar to the situation in which April Glaspie's statements to Saddam Hussein in 1990 will allow the Iraqi ruler mistakenly to believe he can invade Kuwait without American intervention. The U.S. and others will intervene militarily, however, and President Bush will describe it as the beginning of "The New World Order."[5]

1917

▪ February 9: Rep. Oscar Calloway inserts the following statement in the *Congressional Record*:

> In March 1915 the J. P. Morgan interests, the steel, shipbuilding, and powder interests, and their subsidiary organizations got together twelve men high up in the newspaper world and employed them to select the most influential newspapers in the United States and sufficient number of them to control generally the policy of the daily press of the United States. These twelve men worked the problem out by selecting 179

> newspapers, and then began, by an elimination process, to retain only those necessary for the purpose of controlling the general policy of the daily press throughout the country. They found it was only necessary to purchase the control of twenty-five of the greatest newspapers. The twenty-five papers were agreed upon; emissaries were sent to purchase the policy, national and international, of these papers; an agreement was reached; the policy of the papers was bought, to be paid for by the month; an editor was furnished for each paper to properly supervise and edit information regarding the questions of preparedness, militarism, financial policies, and other things of national and international nature considered vital to the interests of the purchasers.

▪ March 24: *The New York Times* on page two prints a telegram from Jacob Schiff describing the Russian Revolution as "what we had hoped and striven for these long years." Schiff had heavily financed Woodrow Wilson's 1912 presidential campaign, and in 1916 Schiff paid Leon Trotsky's way to the U.S. In the *New York Journal–American* (February 3, 1949) one will read:

> Today it is estimated even by Jacob's grandson, John Schiff, a prominent member of New York Society, that the old man sank about $20,000,000 for the final triumph of Bolshevism in Russia. Other New York banking firms also contributed.

▪ August 3: Concerning the First World War, Lord Esher (The Group) writes: "No American is likely to be killed before November. This is unfortunate, as (President) Wilson may require to be steadied before then and only the death of young Americans can ensure him stability." Esher also writes: "No one can truly say that the sufferings of the world have been in vain; for they have regenerated all nations, and ours in particular. Can there be any doubt but that the war has made for progress and not for retrogression?"

Concerning an American view, Lord Esher will write on August 11:

> Mr. Henry Morgenthau asked me to call on him. . . . (He) was one of the principal supporters of President Wilson in the campaign for the Presidency, and he possesses the friendship and confidence of the President. . . . They are ready to sacrifice the lives of American citizens. . . . Mr. Morgenthau realizes the importance upon the morale of the French army and the French people of cementing the Alliance by shedding American blood at the earliest possible moment. If many lives have to be sacrificed, the influence upon the American people can only be beneficent.

Henry Morgenthau, Sr., will be a founding member of the Council on Foreign Relations (CFR). The above quotes come from *Journals and Letters of Reginald, Viscount Esher.*

Col. House, President Wilson's chief advisor and the man primarily responsible for the League of Nations Covenant (influenced by the Fabian Socialists' drafts for the League), would also be largely responsible for the establishment of the Council on Foreign Relations and write in its journal *Foreign Affairs* (June 1923):

> If war had not come in 1914 in fierce and exaggerated form, the idea of an association of nations would probably have remained dormant, for great reforms seldom materialize except during great upheavals. . . . If law and order are good within states (nations), there can be no reason why they should not be good between states (nations).

▪ September: Federal Reserve Bank of New York director William Boyce Thompson contacts the J. P. Morgan bank to give one million dollars of his own money to Aleksandr Kerensky toward the Russian Revolution. After Kerensky falls to the Bolsheviks (Lenin and Trotsky), Thompson will state in an interview in the *New York World* (January 13, 1918):

> Russia is pointing the way to great and sweeping world changes. It is not in Russia alone that the old order is passing. There is a lot of the old order in America, and that is going too. We may just as well open our eyes to it—all of us. The time has come everywhere when affairs must be handled for the benefit of the many—never again for the comparatively few, and what I call legislation by proxy must cease. I'm glad it is so. When I sat and watched those democratic conclaves in Russia, I felt that I would welcome a similar scene in the United States.

In an interview in *The Washington Post* (February 3, 1918), Thompson will advocate that the U.S. should recognize the Bolshevik government. He will also be a founding member of the CFR.

▪ November 7: Lenin leads a successful revolution in Russia to gain communist control. The White Russian General Arsene de Goulevitch would later claim that "over 21 million rubles" had been given to the communists' cause by Lord Milner (The Group).

Lord Milner and Prime Minister David Lloyd George will send Bruce Lockhart to Russia to establish unofficial relations with the Bolsheviks for Britain. Lockhart will become friends with Raymond Robins, a protege of Col. House, after Robins is sent to St. Petersburg in Russia to head the American Red Cross Mission there shortly after the Bolsheviks gain power. In Lockhart's *British Agent* (1933), he will write about Robins:

> Although a rich man himself, he was an anti-capitalist. . . . Hitherto, his two heroes had been [Teddy] Roosevelt and Cecil Rhodes. Now Lenin captured his imagination. . . . Robins was the only man whom Lenin was always willing to see and who ever succeeded in imposing his own personality on the unemotional Bolshevik leader. . . . I returned from our interview to our flat to find an urgent message from Robins requesting me to come to see him at once. . . . When I arrived, he had just finished telephoning Lenin. He had delivered his ultimatum [about Saalkind, Assistant Commissar for Foreign Affairs]. . . . Then the tele-

> phone rang and Robins picked up the receiver. Lenin had capitulated. Saalkind was dismissed from his post.

▪ November 28: After the Bolshevik triumph in Russia, Col. House cables President Wilson from Paris, saying: "There have been cabled over and published here statements made by American papers to the effect that Russia should be treated as an enemy. It is exceedingly important that such criticisms should be suppressed."

▪ Rudyard Kipling is elected a trustee of the Rhodes Trust. His symbol has been the swastika (an emblem that has also been reported as being in the "Skull and Bones" building at Yale University). Kipling was a personal friend of Cecil Rhodes.

1918

▪ Robert Lee Humber will become a Rhodes Scholar and later author of "The Declaration of the Federation of the World," which will be accepted or endorsed by quite a few state bodies, the first of which will be the North Carolina legislature in 1941, and the document will state "that all peoples of the earth should now be united in a commonwealth of nations."[6]

▪ August 7: War Industries Board chairman Bernard Baruch states:

> Every man's life is at the call of the nation and so must be every man's property. We are living today in a highly organized state of socialism. The state is all; the

This is a picture of the key to the city of Seattle. On the right side of the key is a swastika with a right angle like that of the Nazis. The picture was taken July 1995, and the key is on display at Preble Hall, U.S. Naval Academy Museum in Annapolis, Maryland. The plaque under the key says, "Key to the city of Seattle presented to Rear Admiral Charles S. Sperry, USN, by the city on May 23, 1908. Bequeathed by Rear Admiral Sperry."

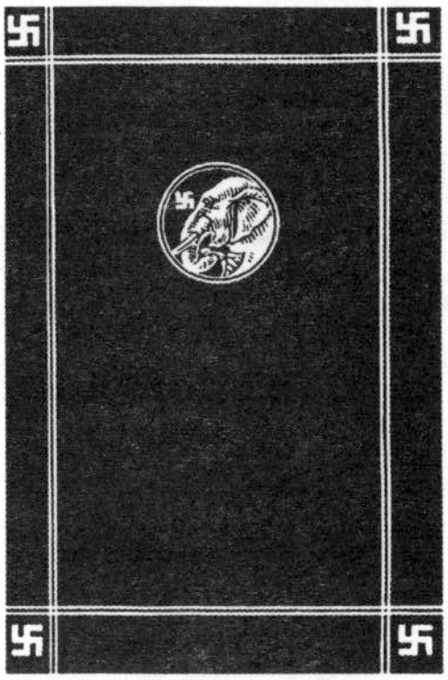

Above is the cover of the New World Edition of the *Works of Rudyard Kipling,* published by Doubleday, Page & Co. for Funk & Wagnalls company. Notice that the angle of the swastika is a right angle like that of the Nazis, not a left angle like that of some Eastern religions.

The swastika with a right angle like that of the Nazis was the symbol of the Citizens National Bank early in the twentieth century.

> individual is of importance only as he contributes to the welfare of the state. His property is only as the state does not need it. He must hold his life and his possessions at the call of the state.

Baruch will be a member of the New York Stock Exchange for many years, and in February 1944 he will make a report to President Roosevelt and Secretary of State James Byrnes concerning the Second World "War and Postwar Plans."

▪ November 8: Charles R. Van Hise, who has been president of the University of Wisconsin, delivers an address to the Wisconsin State Convention of the League to Enforce Peace. The president of the national League to Enforce Peace is former U.S. President William Howard Taft. The title of the address is "The Foundations of a New World Order," in which Charles R. Van Hise states:

> The world has become one body, and no great member of it can proceed independently of the other members. They must act together; and this is possible only through formal treaty covenants.

1919

▪ January: Col. House enters the following statement in his diary:

> I had a heart to heart talk with Clemenceau [Premier of France] about Bolshevism in Russian and its westward march. I made him confess that military inter-

> vention was impossible. . . . Later in the afternoon when Orlando [Premier of Italy] called, I gave him very much the same kind of talk, and he too, agreed with my conclusions. I am trying, and have partially succeeded, to frighten not only the President [Wilson] but the English, French and Italians regarding what might be termed 'the Russian peril.' . . . I would not confess that military intervention was an impossibility, because I believe that it could be successfully accomplished if gone about properly. A voluntary and a mercenary army of very small proportions, equipped with artillery and tanks, would in my opinion do the work.

Col. House here admitted that the spread of the Bolshevik Revolution could have been stopped, but he deliberately misled world leaders, including President Wilson to whom he was chief advisor, to prevent them from stopping it! Think of the millions of people who were eventually slaughtered by the Bolsheviks, and the costly arms race, and the communists' threat of nuclear holocaust hanging over people's heads for most of the past century, and realize how Col. House, as just one member of the power elite, has changed the course of history and has had a tremendous effect upon the lives of all the people of the world.

▪ February 3: The Peace Commission, headed by President Wilson, begins writing draft of League of Nations Covenant.[7] One of the army officers attached to the commission is George Bernard Noble (Rhodes Scholar 1913), who in 1943 will leave a foreign policy commission of the CFR for a position in the State Department.

▪ Lionel Curtis (The Group) founds the Royal Institute of International Affairs (RIIA) which will receive large amounts of funds from the Carnegie Corporation and other branches of the Carnegie Trust. RIIA will also be given considerable financial support from J. P. Morgan and Company, especially a founding grant from Thomas Lamont of that company. Thomas Lamont's son, Corliss, will be a signer of the *Humanist Manifesto* and will be involved with the Institute of Pacific Relations (IPR), whose officers will be dominated by The Group. The influence of communists in the IPR will be well established, and Corliss Lamont will be chairman of the National Council of American-Soviet Friendship (originally beginning in the 1920s as the Friends of the Soviet Union). The IPR will also receive considerable funding from the Rockefeller Foundation, and on the IPR board of directors will be John K. Fairbank (Rhodes Scholar 1929) with Robert Barnett (Rhodes Scholar 1934) being an IPR research associate. A. W. Packard (Rhodes Scholar 1925) will be executive assistant to John D. Rockefeller, Jr.

▪ Henry Allen Moe becomes a Rhodes Scholar, and will later become president of the Guggenheim Foundation, before becoming the first chairman of the National Endowment for the Humanities in 1966.

▪ Crane Brinton becomes a Rhodes Scholar, and he will later be Carroll Quigley's tutor at Harvard University.

He will also be editor of *The American Oxonian* (1936–43) and president of the American Historical Association.

▪ *The New World Order* by Samuel Zane Batten is published by the American Baptist Publication Society. In this book, Batten declares:

> The old order passes from view; the new world rises upon our vision. . . . We have vindicated the right of social control. . . . There must be developed a national spirit of service. . . . Society must break the stranglehold of capitalism. . . . The natural resources of the nation must be socialized. . . . The state must socialize every group. . . . Men must learn to have world patriotism. World patriotism must be a faith. . . . There is no more justice for the claim of absolute sovereignty on the part of a nation than on the part of an individual. . . . The only alternative is *World Federation* . . . with a world parliament, an international court, and an international police force. . . . Men must have an international mind before there can be a world federation. They must see and affirm that above the nation is humanity. Internationalism must first be a religion before it can be a reality and a system.

▪ The third volume of Arthur Calhoun's *A Social History of the American Family* is published and will serve for a number of years as a prominent college social services reference book. In this book, Calhoun proclaims:

> The family goes back to the age of savagery while the state belongs to the age of civilization. The modern

individual is a world citizen, served by the world, and home interests can no longer be supreme. . . . As familism weakens, society has to assume a larger parenthood. The school begins to assume responsibility for the functions thrust upon it. . . . The kindergarten grows downward toward the cradle and there arises talk of neighborhood nurseries. . . . Social centers replace the old time home chimney. . . . The child passes more and more into the custody of community experts. . . . It seems clear that at least in its early stages, socialism will mean an increased amount of social control. . . . We may expect in the socialist commonwealth a system of public educational agencies that will begin with the nursery and follow the individual through life. . . . Those persons that experience alarm at the thought of intrinsic changes in family institutions should remember that in the light of social evolution, nothing is right or valuable in itself.

1920

▪ Stanley Hornbeck (Rhodes Scholar 1904–1907) enters the federal government as special expert for the U.S. Tariff Commission. From 1928 to 1938 he will be chief of Far Eastern Affairs, and from 1939 to 1944 he will be Alger Hiss' superior when Hiss will be special assistant to the Secretary of State. Hornbeck will also be a representative at the Dumbarton Oaks Conference (where Hiss would be executive secretary) early in 1944, and then Hiss would be Secretary-General of the United Nations Conference on International Organization in San Francisco in 1945, where Hiss' special advisor would be Bernadotte

Schmitt (Rhodes Scholar 1905), who in 1943 would become a special consultant to Secretary of War Henry Stimson (a founder of the CFR and a member of "Skull and Bones" who would initiate George Bush into the same society).

In testimony before a congressional committee concerning the Pearl Harbor attack, Admiral J. C. Richardson (who had commanded the Pacific fleet for thirteen months prior to February 1941) said Hornbeck had more to say about the fleet than he did, and President Roosevelt refused to follow the admiral's recommendation to remove the fleet from Hawaii to the west coast of the U.S.

At Hiss' second trial, Hornbeck will acknowledge he had known about Hiss' subversive connections for seven years but didn't tell anyone because, he said, "Hiss was very close to me." Hornbeck will be on the 1964 listing of the American Security Council (ASC) Cold War Advisory Committee, and the ASC will be a supporter of world federalist Thomas Dodd, U.S. Senator from Connecticut. Dodd is a Democrat, and the editor of his state's Democratic Party publication will be George C. Holt (Rhodes Scholar 1931), who will be president of a branch of the United World Federalists.

- John M. Harlan becomes a Rhodes Scholar. He will be a member of the legal firm of Root, Ballantine, Harlan, Bushby, and Palmer in New York City from 1931 to 1954. And from 1955 to 1971 he will be a U.S. Supreme Court Justice.

- *The New World Order* by Frederick Charles Hicks is published. He is law librarian of Columbia University, and in this book, he suggests that among the most powerful few of the Great Powers, the example must be set to "co-operate, here and there, piece by piece, in limiting the exercise of their sovereign rights."

1921

- The Council on Foreign Relations (CFR) is established, largely by Col. House's group, "the Inquiry." It is the American branch of the RIIA, and prior to 1921 was called the Institute of International Affairs. Prof. Quigley will describe the CFR as "a front for J. P. Morgan and Company in association with the very small American Round Table Group."[8] Quigley would continue:

> The board of the CFR have carried ever since the marks of their origin. . . . There grew up in the 20th century a power structure between London and New York which penetrated deeply into university life, the press, and the practice of foreign policy. . . . The American branch of this "English Establishment" exerted much of its influence through five American newspapers (*New York Times, New York Herald Tribune, Christian Science Monitor, Washington Post,* and the late lamented *Boston Evening Transcript).*[9]

One should remember here that in Cecil Rhodes' "Confession of Faith," he wrote that "the [secret] Society should inspire and even own portions of the press, for the press owns the minds of the people."

For many years in the future, John Oakes (Rhodes

Scholar 1934) will be editorial page editor of *The New York Times*. Partners, associates, and employees of J. P. Morgan and Company will load the CFR's board. Whitney Shepardson (Rhodes Scholar 1910) will serve as a director of the CFR from its beginning in 1921 until 1966. He had been assistant to Col. House at the 1918 peace conference and secretary of the League of Nations committee, and he will become director of the Carnegie Corporation British and Colonies fund.

Members of "the Inquiry" included CFR founding member Walter Lippmann (member of the Fabian Society and Intercollegiate Socialist Society) who wrote in *The Political Scene: An Essay on the Victory of 1918* (1919) that World War I in April 1917 "is dissolving into a stupendous revolution" that could hopefully result in "the federation of the world," and future Socialist Party presidential candidate Norman Thomas, who would write:

> The American people will never knowingly adopt Socialism, but under the name of Liberalism they will adopt every fragment of the Socialist program until one day America will be a Socialist nation without knowing how it happened.

▪ Joseph Brandt becomes a Rhodes Scholar. He will later direct the presses of the University of Oklahoma, Princeton University, and the University of Chicago. He will then become president of Henry Holt & Company publishers. (G. D. Gosling, Rhodes Scholar 1931, will be associate editor at Henry Holt & Co.). Henry Holt was a trustee and counselor of the American Society for Psychical Research, which was founded by psychologist William James in 1885. James described the coalescing of children's sensations which are felt as "one great blooming, buzzing confusion." Rhodes Scholar Richard Gardner in the CFR's *Foreign Affairs* (April 1974) will write that "the house of world order will . . . look like a great 'blooming, buzzing confusion' to use William James' famous description of reality," but technological, economic, and political interests will coalesce.

▪ John Tigert (Rhodes Scholar 1904) becomes U.S. Commissioner of Education. He will occupy that position until 1928 when he will become president of the University of Florida until 1947.

1922

▪ Frank Aydelotte (Rhodes Scholar 1905) becomes a trustee of the Carnegie Foundation the year after he becomes president of Swarthmore College, and he will be a member of the CFR for many years. As perhaps the most important member of The Group in the U.S., he is American secretary to the Rhodes Trustees, and will author *The American Rhodes Scholarships* (1946), in which he declares:

> If he [RS] has the capacity for assimilation, if he can become part of what he meets, he may return from Oxford to the United States a citizen of the world. . . . Older [RS] men were often able to assist their young proteges, just back from Oxford, in finding suitable posts in the United States.

Aydelotte will leave Swarthmore College to write this. He will have become director of the Institute for Advanced Study at Princeton, New Jersey, in 1940, and relevant to this is Prof. Carroll Quigley's statement that

> the twentieth century power structure . . . set up in Princeton a reasonable copy of the Round Table Group's chief Oxford headquarters. The copy was called the Institute for Advanced Study and was organized by Abraham Flexner (of the Educational Trust that will direct education in the U.S.), the Carnegie Foundation and Rockefeller's General Education Board. The plans were largely drawn by Tom Jones, one of the Round Table's most active intriguers and foundation administrators.

▪ March 27: *The New York Times* publishes excerpts from a speech by New York City mayor John Hylan concerning the power elite (see pages 226–227 of *Secret Records Revealed).*

▪ December 15: The CFR's journal, *Foreign Affairs*, publishes an article by Philip Kerr (The Group), in which he states:

> Obviously there is going to be no peace or prosperity for mankind as long as (the earth) remains divided into fifty or sixty independent states . . . until some kind of international system is created which will put an end to the diplomatic struggles incident to the attempt of every nation to make itself secure. . . . The

> real problem today is that of [how to get] the world government.

▪ Eddie Eagan becomes a Rhodes Scholar after winning a gold medal in boxing at the 1920 Olympics. He will later become an attorney, and he will coach psychologist Dr. Joyce Brothers on her successful effort to win "The $64,000 Question" in the category of boxing.

1924

▪ January: Reginald McKenna, former Chancellor of the Exchequer in England, tells the stockholders of Midland Bank:

> I am afraid the ordinary citizen will not like to be told that the banks can, and do, create money. . . . And they who control the credit of the nation direct the policy of Governments and hold in the hollow of their hands the destiny of the people.

1925

▪ Charles Saltzman becomes a Rhodes Scholar and will later be a White House aide to President Herbert Hoover, a brigadier general, a vice-president of the New York Stock Exchange, a partner in Goldman Sachs (international bankers) and an Undersecretary of State for Administration.

1926

▪ *Holism and Evolution* by Jan Christiaan Smuts (The Group) is published describing "the foundations of a new order of the universe." Smuts' holism is a synthesis or unity of parts. He drafted many of the clauses of the League of Nations Covenant (his plan for the League of Nations was published December 16, 1918), and he said, "Europe is being liquidated and the League of Nations must be heir to this great estate." Smuts would also be one of the drafters of the preamble for the United Nations Charter, and his holistic approach would be adopted by Alger Hiss. Smuts would likewise influence Frederick (Fritz) Perls, the principal founder of Gestalt therapy, which is a holistic, self-actualizing approach emphasizing the here-and-now.

1928

▪ William Paley (CFR) will begin the Columbia Broadcasting System (CBS) and hire Sigmund Freud's nephew, Edward Bernays, as his chief advisor. In this same year, Bernays authors *Propaganda*, in which he reveals:

> Those who manipulate the organized habits and opinions of the masses constitute an invisible government which is the true ruling power of the country. . . . It remains a fact that in almost every act of our daily lives, whether in the sphere of politics or business, in our social conduct or our ethical thinking, we are dominated by the relatively small number of persons. . . . It is they who pull the wires which control the public mind, who harness old social forces and contrive new ways to bind and guide the world. . . . As civilization has become more complex, and as the need for invisible government has been increasingly dem-

> onstrated, the technical means have been invented and developed by which opinion may be regimented.

According to Bernays, politicians and businessmen should take "a survey of public desires and demands" in order to say, "I must lead the people. Am I not their servant?" Does this sound similar to what Ross Perot will say in 1992? (See *The Network of Power and Part II of The New World Order: Chronology and Commentary,* by Dennis Laurence Cuddy and Robert Henry Goldsborough, published by The American Research Foundation, Baltimore, MD.)

▪ *The Open Conspiracy: Blue Prints for a World Revolution* by H. G. Wells is published. He declares that

> the political world of the Open Conspiracy must weaken, efface, incorporate and supersede existing governments.... The Open Conspiracy is the natural inheritor of socialist and communist enthusiasms; it may be in control of Moscow before it is in control of New York....

1929

▪ July: According to Sir Francis Wylie's recollections (later published by the Rhodes Trust), in this month there is a garden party given by Lord Astor (The Group) and Lady Astor for Rhodes Scholars and their wives (almost three hundred) "with Bernard Shaw as an extra attraction." Shaw is a Fabian Socialist who wrote in 1928 (the year **before** this garden party) *The Intelligent Woman's Guide to Socialism and Capitalism,* in which he stated:

> . . . under Socialism you would not be allowed to be poor. You would be forcibly fed, clothed, lodged, taught, and employed whether you liked it or not. If it were discovered that you had not the character and industry enough to be worth all this trouble, you might possibly be executed in a kindly manner. . . .

▪ *Individualism, Old and New* by John Dewey is published, in which he predicts: "We are in for some kind of socialism, call it by whatever name we please, and no matter what it will be called when it is realized." Dewey will co-author the 1933 *Humanist Manifesto,* and he is the "Father of Progressive Education," which will gain greater and greater influence in American schools throughout the century.

In *The New Republic* (December 5, 1928), Dewey had written about

> . . . the marvelous development of progressive educational ideas and practices under the fostering care of the Bolshevist government. . . . The task of the school [in the U.S.S.R.] is to counteract and transform those domestic neighborhood tendencies . . . the influence of home and Church. . . . The institution of the family is being sapped indirectly rather than by frontal attack. . . . All sorts of groups are instituted that militate against the primary social importance of the family unit. In consequence, to anyone who looks at the matter cold-bloodedly, free from sentimental associations clustering about the historic family institution, a most interesting sociological experimentation is taking place. . . .

▪ October: The stock market crashes, setting off the Great Depression. In Congress in the early 1930s, Rep. Louis McFadden will explain that this "was not accidental. It was a carefully contrived occurrence. . . . The international bankers sought to bring about a condition of despair here so they might emerge rulers of us all." There were at least two attempts (by gunfire) on McFadden's life. In *F.D.R.: My Exploited Father-in-Law,* Curtis Dall (member of the New York Stock Exchange, a syndicate manager for Lehman Brothers, and husband of Anna Roosevelt) will later explain that the crash

> was the calculated "shearing" of the public by the World-Money powers, triggered by the planned sudden shortage of the supply of call money in the New York money market. . . . For a long time I felt that FDR had developed many thoughts and ideas that were his own to benefit this country, the U.S.A. But he didn't. Most of his thoughts, his political "ammunition," as it were, was carefully manufactured for him in advance by the CFR–One-World Money group. . . . It appears to me that politics is the gentle art of having to pretend to be something that you know you are not, for vote-catching purposes, while being aided by our press. . . . Usually, carefully screened leading "actors" are picked for *both major parties.* . . . It is desirable for (candidates) to have great *personal ambition* and, perchance, to be *vulnerable to blackmail* . . . (Col. House knew Woodrow Wilson was vulnerable to blackmail) . . . for some past occurrences; hence, someone not apt to become too independent in time. . . .

▪ The (Owen D.) Young Plan concerning the war reparations problem is developed, and results in the establishment of the Bank for International Settlements (BIS) in 1930. The primary influence on this plan is J. P. Morgan and Company, and the BIS will be the central bank of the world for all nations' central banks (e.g., Federal Reserve, Bundesbank, etc.). Concerning the BIS, Prof. Quigley will write in *Tragedy and Hope* about the plan

> to create a world system of financial control in private hands able to dominate the political system of each country and the economy of the world as a whole. This system was to be controlled in a feudalist fashion by the central banks of the world acting in concert, by secret agreements arrived at in frequent meetings and conferences. The apex of the systems was to be the Bank for International Settlements in Basel, Switzerland, a private bank owned and controlled by the world's central banks which were themselves private corporations. Each central bank . . . sought to dominate its government by its ability to control Treasury loans, to manipulate foreign exchanges, to influence the level of economic activity in the country, and to influence cooperative politicians by subsequent economic rewards in the business world.[10]

Owen D. Young is a CFR director from 1927 to 1940.

▪ John K. Fairbank becomes a Rhodes Scholar and from 1947 to 1951 will be trustee of the radical leftist Institute of Pacific Relations. He will also be president of the American Historical Association.

▪ Malcolm MacIntyre becomes a Rhodes Scholar and will later become president of Eastern Airlines and executive vice-president of Martin Marietta.

1930

▪ June: *The New York Times* publishes an article quoting Rep. Louis McFadden (chairman of the House Committee on Banking and Currency) as saying:

> The Federal Reserve Bank of New York is eager to enter into close relationship with the Bank for International Settlements.... The conclusion is impossible to escape that the State and Treasury Departments are willing to pool the banking systems of Europe and America, setting up a world financial power independent of and above the Government of the United States.... The United States under present conditions will be transformed from the most active of manufacturing nations into a consuming and importing nation with a balance of trade against it.

1931

▪ June: Arnold Toynbee (The Group) delivers a speech to the Institute for the Study of International Affairs at Copenhagen in which he explains:

> We are at present working discreetly with all our might to wrest this mysterious force called sovereignty out of the clutches of the local nation states of the world. All the time we are denying with our lips what we are doing with our hands, because to impugn the sover-

eignty of the local nation states of the world is still a heresy for which a statesman or publicist can perhaps not quite be burned at the stake but certainly be ostracized or discredited.

—*International Affairs* (journal of the Royal Institute of International Affairs), November 1931, "The Trend of International Affairs Since the War"

▪ Fowler Hamilton becomes a Rhodes Scholar and in the late 1930s will be a U.S. Assistant Attorney-General. President Kennedy will appoint him to be the first head of the Agency for International Development.

1932

▪ Charles Hitch becomes a Rhodes Scholar and will later develop in the U.S. the controversial Planning-Programming-Budgeting System (PPBS). Hitch came to England as a Rhodes Scholar at a time when the British Political and Economic Planning (PEP) organization had recently been instituted. PEP was a Fabian-sponsored organization. In the May 3, 1934, *Congressional Record,* Congressman Louis McFadden will quote PEP member Israel Moses Sieff as saying: "Let us go slowly for a while, until we can see how our plan works out in America." The "plan" to which Sieff referred is the New Deal, which was drafted in the U.S. by the National Planning Association (NPA). The NPA is, and the Committee for Economic Development (CED, founded in 1941) will be, descendants of PEP. In the 1990s, the CED will be composed of some two hundred and fifty business leaders and educators, almost one hundred of whom will be CFR members.

▪ The Rockefeller Foundation gives the RIIA a grant of eight thousand pounds a year for five years to advance the study-group method of research. The grants will be extended for five more years in 1937.

1933

▪ May 4: Rep. Louis McFadden in the *Congressional Record* refers to "the international bankers who own and control the Federal Reserve Board and the Federal Reserve banks."

▪ *The Shape of Things to Come* by H. G. Wells is published, in which he predicts a Second World War will begin in or about 1940, originating from a German-Polish dispute. Wells says the plan for the "Modern World-State" would succeed on its third attempt (about 1980), and come out of something that would occur in Basra, Iraq. At this point, he states, "Russia is ready to assimilate. Is eager to assimilate." Although world government "had been plainly coming for some years, although it had been endlessly feared and murmured against, it found no opposition prepared anywhere."

▪ November 21: President Franklin Roosevelt writes a letter to Col. House in which he relates that he has just been talking with Jack Morgan (J. P. Morgan's son), and then he remarks:

> The real truth of the matter is, as you and I know, that a financial element in the larger centers has owned government ever since the days of Andrew Jackson—and I am not wholly excepting the Administration of W. W. (Woodrow Wilson).[11]

Years later, President Franklin Roosevelt will be quoted as having said, "In politics, nothing happens by accident. If it happens, it was planned that way." Remember this especially regarding the presidential elections of 1912 and 1992.

1934

▪ John M. Templeton becomes a Rhodes Scholar, and will later endow the "Templeton Prize for Progress in Religion" which will be awarded in his name each year. The prize of one million dollars will be awarded to those advancing "the world's understanding of God or spirituality," such as Mother Teresa (1973), Dr. Billy Graham (1982), Aleksandr Solzhenitsyn (1983), Muslim Dr. Inamullah Khan (1988), Rabbi Immanuel Jakobovits (1991), Bill Bright (1996), and Hindu religious activist Pandurang Shastri Athavale (1997). Charles Colson's 1993 award will be announced at a press conference at the Church Center for the United Nations, and the public ceremony will be held at the Rockefeller Chapel of the University of Chicago during the centenary meeting of the Parliament of World Religions. Templeton will be knighted in 1987 by Queen Elizabeth II for his benefactions, and then he will be known as Sir John Templeton.

▪ Richard Goodwin becomes a Rhodes Scholar and will

later teach economics at Harvard University. However, he will be denied tenure there after Daniel Boorstin (Rhodes Scholar 1934 and a member of Oxford's Marxists' October Club) willingly testifies before the U.S. House Un-American Activities Committee in 1950, saying that Goodwin and others had been members of the Communist Party.

▪ *Experiment in Autobiography* by H. G. Wells is published, in which he states:

> The organization of this that I call the Open Conspiracy . . . which will ultimately supply teaching, coercive and directive public services to the whole world, is the immediate task before all rational people. . . . A planned world-state is appearing at a thousand points. . . . Plans for political synthesis seem to grow bolder and more extensive. . . . There must be a common faith and law for mankind. . . . The main battle is an educational battle.

1935

▪ February 27: H. G. Wells writes to President Roosevelt telling him that he is coming to the United States and would like to talk with him. Wells concludes the letter by saying, "My address will be c/o The Chase National Bank, Park Avenue, N.Y.C." The Chase National Bank is owned by Rockefeller.

▪ Donald Wheeler becomes a Rhodes Scholar and will later join the OSS (forerunner of the CIA).

1936

▪ July 26: *The New York Times* quotes Joseph Kennedy (the future President Kennedy's father and former chairman of the Securities and Exchange Commission) as stating:

> Fifty men have run America, and that's a high figure. . . . I don't see how anybody giving any thought to the trends all over the world can help but feel there is something in the air in the advancement of some new social order. . . . That is why I feel it is of the greatest importance to re-elect Mr. Roosevelt.

In Kennedy's *I'm For Roosevelt* (1936), Kennedy would propose that "an organized functioning society requires a planned economy. . . . Otherwise, there results a haphazard and inefficient method of social control. . . ." Regarding this statement, Richard Whalen in *The Founding Father* (1964) will remark: "He omitted a definition of 'social control,' a euphemism for state coercion. . . . It called to mind countries where efficiency flourished at the expense of freedom."

▪ July 29: *The New Republic* publishes a statement by philosopher of British Socialism Harold Laski regarding the "Conclusions and Recommendations" (1934) of the Commission on Social Studies of the American Historical Association. Laski characterizes the report as follows: ". . . at bottom, and stripped of its carefully neutral phrases, the report is an educational program for a Socialist America."

▪ Dyke Brown becomes a Rhodes Scholar, and in this year

the Ford Foundation is begun. He will help write *The Gaither Report* and become one of the Ford Foundation's first vice-presidents. In the fall of 1953, Ford Foundation president H. Rowan Gaither will admit to Norman Dodd (staff director of the Congressional Special Committee to Investigate Tax-Exempt Foundations):

> Of course, you know that we at the executive level here were, at one time or another, active in either the OSS, the State Department, or the European Economic Administration. During those times, and without exception, we operated under directives issued by the White House. We are continuing to be guided by just such directives. . . . The substance (of these directives) was to the effect that we should make every effort to so alter life in the United States as to make possible a comfortable merger with the Soviet Union.

- Murat Williams becomes a Rhodes Scholar and will later be U.S. Ambassador to El Salvador.

1937

- Frank Taplin becomes a Rhodes Scholar and later president and CEO of the Metropolitan Opera.

1939

- The Group dominates *The* (London) *Times*, and in *Oxford As It Was and As It Is Today*, published this year, author Christopher Hobhouse writes:

> It is the Editor of *The Times* and his circle of associates—men whom the public voice has called to no office and entrusted with no responsibility. These indi-

> viduals elect to consider themselves the powers behind the scenes. The duty of purveying honest news is elevated in their eyes into the prerogative of dictating opinion. It is at All Souls (College, Oxford University) that they meet to decide just how little they will let their readers know.

▪ *Union Now: A Proposal for a Federal Union of the Leading Democracies* by Clarence Streit (The Group, and RS 1918) is published. Advertisements for the book are run in the CFR's *Foreign Affairs*, and it is favorably reviewed by Philip Kerr (Lord Lothian) in *The Christian Science Monitor* (May 6, 1939).[12] The book is distributed to various educational institutions by the Carnegie Foundation. Streit had been the League of Nations correspondent of the *New York Times* (1929–38), and his Union Now organization (The Association to Unite the Democracies) will be incorporated in 1940 as Federal Union. An offshoot of Federal Union will be the Atlantic Union Committee with Streit on its board and the following Rhodes Scholars on its Council: Frank Aydelotte, William Yandell Elliott, and John Nason. Similar organizations are or will be: the Foundation for World Government with Stringfellow Barr (Rhodes Scholar 1917) as president and Scott Buchanan (Rhodes Scholar 1917) as secretary; United World Federalists with Vernon Nash (Rhodes Scholar 1916) as vice-president, G. C. Holt (Rhodes Scholar 1931) on the national executive council, and Robert Lee Humber (Rhodes Scholar 1918) on the national advisory board; and Union for Democratic Action with David C. Williams (Rhodes Scholar 1932) as a European director.

▪ *The New World Order* by socialist H. G. Wells is published, in which he claims:

> It is the system of nationalist individualism that has to go. . . . We are living in the end of the sovereign states. . . . In the great struggle to evoke a Westernized World Socialism, contemporary governments may vanish. . . . Countless people . . . will hate the new world order . . . and will die protesting against it.[13]

▪ *World Order (Civitas Dei)* by Lionel Curtis (The Group) is published. This 985-page volume will be called the foundation of all thought on the design of a new order. It examines human society and concludes that a working system must mean the organization of all human society into one commonwealth.

▪ October 28: Future Secretary of State John Foster Dulles (CFR member) delivers a speech (reported in *The New York Times*, October 29) to the YMCA, in which he states:

> (There must be) some dilution of sovereignty, to the immediate disadvantage of those nations which now possess the preponderance of power . . . the establishment of a common money, might be vested in a body created by and responsible to the principle of trading and investing peoples. This would deprive our government of exclusive control over a national money.

▪ Philip Kaiser (Rhodes Scholar 1936) becomes a member of the board of governors of the Federal Reserve System at a very young age, and will serve in that capacity until 1942. He will become U.S. Ambassador to the Republic of Senegal and the Islamic Republic of Mauritania, 1961–64. He will then become Minister to the American Embassy in London, 1964–69. Following this, he will become chairman of Encyclopaedia Britannica International Ltd., 1969–75. He will then be U.S. Ambassador to the People's Republic of Hungary, 1977–80, and Austria, 1980–81. He will also be a CFR member.

▪ Morris Abram becomes a Rhodes Scholar. He will later be national president of the American Jewish Committee, president of Brandeis University, chief U.S. delegate to the Conference on Security and Cooperation in Europe (CSCE), Ambassador to the U.N. (European office in Geneva), member of the CFR and Institute for International Education, and on the board of directors of the 20th Century Fund.

1941

▪ In volume 28 of *The American Oxonian*, one finds Edward Porter (Rhodes Scholar 1913) stating:

> The Nazis are the only people who have ever made a thorough and organized effort to put brains into government, and unless we learn from them as they have from us, this war is going to be a greater waste of time and effort than the first one.

▪ *The City of Man* is co-authored by a number of people including Frank Aydelotte (Rhodes Scholar 1905) and

William Yandell Elliott (Rhodes Scholar 1919), professor of government at Harvard University. In this book one reads:

> Universal peace can be founded only on the unity of man under one law and one government. . . . All states, deflated and disciplined, must align themselves under the law of the world-state . . . the new order . . . when the heresy of nationalism is conquered and the absurd architecture of the present world is finally dismantled. . . . And there must be a common creed . . . or ethico-religious purpose.

■ November 25: Secretary of War Henry Stimson writes in his diary:

> President Roosevelt brought up the event that we are likely to be attacked perhaps (as soon as) next Mon-

Japanese May Strike Over Weekend!

The Honolulu Sunday Advertiser

FINAL EDITION

KURUSU BLUNTLY WARNED NATION READY FOR BATTLE

Mexican Cop Says Torrance Slayer Of Wife

Leaders Call Troops Back In Singapore

Will Santa Fit The Plane?

Nazis Clamp Curfew Over Montmarte

Foreign Affairs Expert Attacks Tokio Madness

British Reveal Naval Help To Reds In Arctic

Above is the front page from *The Honolulu Advertiser* for November 30, 1941, announcing that the "Japanese May Strike Over Weekend!"

> day, for the Japanese are notorious for making an attack without warning, and the question was how we should maneuver them into the position of firing the first shot.

The next day (November 26), according to Gregory Douglas' *Gestapo Chief: The 1948 Interrogation of Heinrich Müller*, Prime Minister Winston Churchill calls FDR and informs him that the Japanese will attack Pearl Harbor on December 8 (that is Japanese time, which would be December 7 in the U.S.). The front page headline for *The Honolulu Advertiser* on November 30 reads "Japan May Strike Over Weekend!" And on December 5, Sir Julian Huxley (a Fabian Socialist who will be the first Director-General of UNESCO, and who will sign *Humanist Manifesto II*) states that he hopes America and Japan will be at war "next week" (Sunday, December 7, is the first day of the next week, and the day Pearl Harbor is attacked by the Japanese). Huxley is perhaps a member of Churchill's "secret circle," as mentioned in Churchill's October 15 letter to H. G. Wells saying: "It is quite impossible for me to discuss these matters outside the secret circle."

According to *Time* (February 17, 1997), Pamela Churchill (wife of Prime Minister Churchill's son, Randolph) had an affair with Averell Harriman, top U.S. envoy in Britain, "from whom she channeled intelligence information to her father-in-law to help draw the U.S. into the [Second World] War." The *Time* article also will say that at a one-day fundraiser in 1992, she will raise more than three million dollars for presidential candidate Bill Clinton.

1942

▪ March 16: *Time* publishes "American Malvern" concerning a meeting last week of the Federal Council of Churches. Future Secretary of State John Foster Dulles was chairman at the meeting, which called for a world government of delegated powers, strong immediate limitations on national sovereignty, international control of all armies and navies, an international court with adequate jurisdiction, a universal system of money, progressive elimination of all tariff and quota restrictions on world trade, an international bank, and worldwide freedom of immigration. World Council of Churches co-secretary Dr. William Paton told the meeting, "Collectivism is coming, whether we like it or not."

▪ *Post-War Worlds* by P. E. Corbett (The Group) is published as part of the IPR "Inquiry Series." The author states:

> It must be recognized that the law of nations takes precedence over national law. . . . A world association binding together and coordinating regional groupings of states may evolve toward one universal federal government. . . . The process will have to be assisted by the deletion of the nationalistic material employed in educational textbooks and its replacement by material explaining the benefits of wider association. . . . World government is the ultimate aim, but there is more chance of attaining it by gradual development. . . . Men . . . are looking to . . . common economic agencies for advice and control. . . . An Economic and Financial Organization, embracing Trade, Development,

> and Migration Commissions, and a Central Bank. The functions of these institutions . . . would be to regulate the production and distribution of raw materials and food, control the flow of inter-regional investment and migration, etc.[14]

The European Community and NAFTA in the future seem to be the type of regional economic groupings Corbett is referring to that can be linked and form the basis for the establishment of a World (Socialist) Government to administer them. And perhaps the "Economic and Financial Organization" alluded to above could be the World Economic Development Congress which would be founded in 1989. At WEDC's first major international conference, to be held in 1992 and dedicated to "Building the Integrated Global Economy," will be keynote speakers Margaret Thatcher, Trilateralist and CFR member Henry Kissinger, and GATT (General Agreement on Tariffs and Trade) director general Arthur Dunkel. Session moderators at the WEDC 1992 Congress will include Charles Dallara (managing director of J. P. Morgan and Company) and CFR member Lloyd Cutler. Rhodes Scholar and Trilateralist Lester Thurow will be a speaker at the session titled "Global Work Force of the Future." In 1993, the WEDC will hold a global meeting in Washington, D.C., as well as regional meetings in Hamburg, London, and Manila; and WEDC will convene the Congress of the Americas, in Guadalajara in 1994.

▪ *The Last Train from Berlin* by Howard K. Smith (Rhodes Scholar 1937 and elected president of the socialist Labour

Club at Oxford in 1939) is published, in which he remarks that "Russia looked better the longer I stayed and the more I saw." In 1949, he will author *The State of Europe,* in which he will declare that the communist regimes of Eastern Europe

> have been in at least the social and economic realms, an outstanding success. . . . The maintenance of the system of private enterprise is not only becoming technically less possible; it is rapidly losing its last moral justifications. . . . The Soviets have seen the clear fact that the survival of capitalism is impossible in Europe. They have certainly brought to the common man of Europe a richer life.

1943

▪ August 26: The *Chicago Daily Tribune* publishes an article, "Mr. Rhodes' Agents," in which is written:

> Rep. J. W. Fulbright of Arkansas is the author of the slick termed resolution seeking to pledge congress in advance to a world super-government. He is a Rhodes scholar. Rep. Robert Hale of Maine is touring the country, making speeches on behalf of a similar resolution pending in the Senate. He is another Rhodes scholar.

1944

▪ *The Time for Decision* by American government official Sumner Welles is published. It is important to remember that Welles is writing this long before the Nazis are defeated, and in chapter nine he reveals that the German General Staff "made detailed plans for a later renewal of its attempt to dominate the world . . . when the favorable moment arrives . . . (perhaps) two generations from now" (1990s). Welles goes on to say "half the mechanism is secret and will so remain," and involves the theory of

> indirect complicity . . . in three principal ways: (a) It will try to create doubts among the people of each country as to the ability, integrity, wisdom, or loyalty of their leading statesmen; (b) in critical moments it will attempt to paralyze or to diminish the capacity for cool thinking by the people as a whole; and (c) it will search each country for men who, through ambition, vanity, or personal interest, will be disposed to serve the causes. . . . Agents of the German General Staff have already been naturalized, usually in two successive countries, so that their future activities will be less suspect. The majority of them are being trained to appear as men of large commercial or financial interests . . . over a period of years (gaining) a controlling influence in labor unions, in the banking world, in Chambers of Commerce, and, through these channels, an indirect influence in the press. . . . When the right time comes, stimulate internal dissension sufficiently to destroy the morale of the people in those countries marked as victims.

▪ *Federation: The Coming Structure of World Government* is published, including an essay, "The Political Basis of Federation" by William P. Maddox (Rhodes Scholar 1922), who proclaims:

> There is no true federation unless the central author-

> ity possesses a power of decision and action independent of the wills of the separate governments. . . . The second basis of power is financial . . . through the power of direct taxation, rather than through the device of levies upon state governments. . . . The central government must maintain a military monopoly.[15]

Other essayists write about "the new world order," "an outgrown nationalism," "the dying nationalistic century," and "our national-state system as outmoded as were the horse and buggy."[16]

▪ April 10–15: *Senior Scholastic* publishes the following concerning a student poll:

> It has been said that, if we are to establish a successful world organization of nations to prevent war, the American people must be willing to make the necessary personal and national sacrifices. In order to establish a world organization of nations, would you yourself, as an American citizen, be willing or not willing: to allow foreign goods to come into this country, free of tariff duties, and compete with the things we grow or make here, provided all other member nations of the world organization would grant us equal privileges; to pool our army, navy, and air forces with those of other nations in order to establish a strong world police force under international control; to see a "flag of the world" fly above the Stars and Stripes?

1945

▪ January: *The American Oxonian* publishes an article by

Sir Francis Wylie (first Oxford secretary to the Rhodes Trust), in which he reveals that a Rhodes Scholarship

> is not an educational endowment as ordinarily understood . . . but to encourage in the rising generation of English-speaking people a particular outlook on the problems of the world—to give them, in fact, a political bias.

▪ April 25–June 26: The U.N. Charter is drafted in San Francisco and will become effective on October 24.[17] A technical expert to the U.S. delegation there is Clyde Eagleton (Rhodes Scholar 1914), who had been assistant secretary at the August 21 to October 7, 1944, Dumbarton Oaks discussions leading to the San Francisco conference. Eagleton would also be a legal columnist for the *U.N. World.* Likewise at the conference is *Christian Science Monitor* editor Erwin Canham (Rhodes Scholar 1926), who would write that his predecessor, Frederick Dixon, was "on intimate terms with Colonel Edward M. House." Canham would also note that Lord Lothian (Philip Kerr) wrote an editorial page column for the *Monitor*, and the latter was a trustee and secretary to the Rhodes Trust. Lord Lothian was also a member of The Group. And Canham will become president of the U.S. Chamber of Commerce and of the American Society of Newspaper Editors, as well as chairman of a Rhodes Scholarship Selection Committee.

▪ Rockefeller Foundation medical director Alan Gregg tours various institutions that have been involved in war medicine to see if any group will commit to undertake the kind of social psychiatry that had been developed by the army during wartime (e.g., cultural psychiatry for the analysis of the enemy mentality), and see if it could be relevant for the civilian society. This will lead to a Rockefeller grant that will result in the birth of the Tavistock Institute of Human Relations in London 1947. Relevant to this is *Science of Coercion: Communication Research and Psychological Warfare 1945–1960* by Christopher Simpson (published in 1994 by Oxford University Press), in which he states:

> I first discuss U.S. psychological warfare prior to 1945, stressing the early work of noted communication theorists Harold Lasswell and Walter Lippmann and the pioneer studies underwritten by the Rockefeller Foundation. . . . Lasswell and Lippmann advocated . . . a particular social order in the United States and the world in which forceful elites necessarily ruled in the interest of their vision of the greater good. U.S.-style consumer democracy was simply a relatively benign system for engineering mass consent for the elite's authority. . . . Harold Lasswell had the ear of (Rockefeller) Foundation administrator John Marshall. . . . The elite of U.S. society ("those who have money to support research," as Lasswell bluntly put it) should systematically manipulate mass sentiment. [For more on Tavistock, look under 1977.]

▪ May: *International Conciliation* (published by the Carnegie Endowment for International Peace) prints

"The International Court of the United Nations Organization: A Consensus of American and Canadian Views," in which is stated:

> The twenty-five Regional Group Conferences (of the American and Canadian Bar Associations) held throughout the United States and Canada revealed a remarkable agreement. . . . By a great preponderance the opinion was shown to be that an international court of justice should form an integral part of the United Nations Organization, (and) that every effort should be made to extend the compulsory jurisdiction of the Court with reference to legal disputes.

▪ June 28: President Harry Truman states: "We are going to have to ratify this (U.N.) Constitution of San Francisco. . . . It will be just as easy for nations to get along in a republic of the world as it is for us to get along in the republic of the United States." On the same day, regarding the charter of the World Court also signed in San Francisco, Truman states that if two American states have a quarrel, "they bring suit in the Supreme Court and abide by its decision. There isn't any reason in the world why we can't do that internationally."

1946

▪ January: The *NEA Journal* publishes "The Teacher and World Government" by Joy Elmer Morgan (editor of the *NEA Journal*, 1921–55), in which he states: "At the very top of all the agencies which will assure the coming of world government must stand the school, the teacher, and the organized profession." Morgan has already called in the December 1942 *NEA Journal* for a world system of money and credit, a uniform system of weights and measures, a world police force, and other agencies.

▪ April 6: President Truman indicates that he believes a new course should be instituted in the high school curriculum to prepare youth for world citizenship.

▪ Frederick Hovde (Rhodes Scholar 1929–32) becomes president of Purdue University, occupying that position until 1971. During that time, he will also be a consultant to the National War College (1953–55). And he will be a director of General Electric Company, as well as a trustee of the Carnegie Fund for the Advancement of Teaching.

▪ *The American Rhodes Scholarships: A Review of the First Forty Years* is published, listing all of the American Rhodes Scholars since the beginning of the scholarships in 1904. The book is by Frank Aydelotte, first American Secretary to the Rhodes Trustees, and he lists over eleven hundred American Rhodes Scholars since 1904, with 387 in the field of education, 243 in law, 128 in business or banking, 56 in government service, 40 in journalism or media, and 26 in the ministry or religious work.

▪ The World Movement for World Federal Government is formed, and its philosophy will be expressed in its Montreaux Declaration next year.

▪ September 23: Assistant Secretary of State (1945–47) William Benton addresses the National Commission on

Educational, Scientific, and Cultural Cooperation, and states:

> How will UNESCO project its policies within the United States? . . . You are expected to help carry out the UNESCO program within the United States. . . . We are at the beginning of a long process of breaking down the walls of national sovereignty. . . . You are in touch with our schools and colleges, and with organized private groups throughout this country; it will be your task and your opportunity to bring these organizations, and the tens of millions of individual human beings which comprise them, into active participation in the work of UNESCO. . . . The peoples of the world . . . wish to break down . . . the vested interest of the group or of the country operating against the interests of the many and the world. . . .

Benton had been vice-president of the University of Chicago until 1945. He has also been chairman of the board of *Encyclopaedia Britannica* since 1943, and will continue in that position until 1973. In addition, he will be a U.S. Senator from 1949 to 1953.

1947

- February: The uniting conference of various groups of federalists in America is held at Asheville, North Carolina, from which will emerge United World Federalists, USA (later called the World Federalist Association). Grenville Clark becomes the new organization's vice-president, and in 1950 authors *Plan for Peace*, stating:

> The thesis of this volume is that disarmament is the crux of the problem of world order, and that only disarmament in all arms and by all nations will suffice . . . creation of a limited world government . . . including a plan for disarmament by stages and for a United Nations Peace Force.

Rhodes Scholar Robert Lee Humber will be another early vice-president of the United World Federalists.

▪ July 9: U.S. Rep. Richard Nixon introduces House Concurrent Resolution 68 indicating

> . . . that it is the sense of Congress that the President of the United States should immediately take the initiative in calling a General Conference of the United Nations pursuant to [U.N.] Article 109 for the purpose of making the United Nations capable of enacting, interpreting, and enforcing world law to prevent war.

▪ Amos Jordan becomes a Rhodes Scholar. As a lieutenant colonel, he (and CFR "Wise Man" Paul Nitze) will be a contributor to William Frye's *A United Nations Peace Force* (published in 1957 under the auspices of the Carnegie Endowment for International Peace). Others who become Rhodes Scholars in this year are the following: Frank Barnett (will become president of the National Strategy Information Center and a visiting faculty member at the National War College in Washington, D.C., where he will denounce "crackpots" who hunt for "pinkos" in local colleges in 1961), Nicholas Katzenbach (will become U.S. Attorney General and Undersecretary of State), Edmund

Dews (will be with the Rand Corporation), James Hester (will be president of New York University), James Engle (will be Foreign Service Officer), Richard Nolte (will be a Ford Foundation Fellow and Ambassador to the United Arab Republic), Bernard Rogers (will be a brigadier general commandant at the U.S. Military Academy), Robert Porter (will be a dean at Yale University), and Wilfred Kluss. Kluss will be with Standard Oil as well as Morgan, Stanley and Co. investment bankers. He will also be with the Economic Cooperation Administration as will other Rhodes Scholars including John Cassels, Lincoln Gordon, Harlan Cleveland, B. E. L. Timmons, A. B. Daspit, Felix Shafner, and S. J. Hyning, Jr. The focus of economic cooperation would be in Europe, where Rhodes Scholars R. L. Guthrie, N. H. Mitchell, and John Golay are all with the Allied High Commission.

▪ The leftist organization Americans for Democratic Action (ADA) is founded. David C. Williams (Rhodes Scholar 1932) will be its international director. He is a member of the Fabian Society who will write speeches for Hubert Humphrey, and who will say the "ADA is not a political party. It operates very much as the early Fabian Society did seeking to permeate the existing parties."

▪ Robert Marston becomes a Rhodes Scholar. He will later become dean of the medical school of the University of Mississippi, director of the National Institutes of Health, and president of the University of Florida.

▪ May 13: Winston Churchill pronounces:

> Unless some effective world supergovernment for the purposes of preventing war, can be set up and begin to reign, the prospects for peace and human progress are dark and doubtful. . . . But let there be no mistake upon one point. Without a United Europe there is no prospect of world government. It is the urgent and indispensable step toward the realization of that goal.

- *Peace or Anarchy* by Cord Meyer, Jr., is published. Meyer has been a member of the Scroll and Key society at Yale University, as has Dean Acheson. Meyer has become the first president of United World Federalists, and will work for the CIA from 1951 to 1977. He is also a CFR member, and in this book, he advocates that

> the U.N. must be given the constitutional authority to maintain security through laws which call for obedience from the individual inhabitants of the world as their first duty and which no national government can override. . . . Disarmament must be enforced by law and the possession of war-making power by national governments prohibited. . . . So long as the present sovereign state system exists, each government will continue to distort the education of its youth with nationalistic propaganda. . . . Many of these proposals may appear unpatriotic or even treasonous to those who identify patriotism with the worship of American military power.

1948

- July: The CFR's *Foreign Affairs* publishes "A New World

Takes Shape" by Sir Harold Butler (The Group), in which he asks:

> How far can the life of nations, which for centuries have thought of themselves as distinct and unique, be merged with the life of other nations? How far are they prepared to sacrifice a part of their sovereignty without which there can be no effective economic or political union? . . . Out of the prevailing confusion a new world is taking shape . . . which may point the way toward the new order.[18]

▪ The Group controls *The* (London) *Times,* which in turn controls *Encyclopaedia Britannica,* whose head will be Mortimer Adler, who will with Robert Hutchins, Rexford Tugwell, Stringfellow Barr (Rhodes Scholar 1917), and others, co-author this year the *Preliminary Draft of a World Constitution.* It advocates regional federation on the way toward world federation or world government. The constitution provides for a "World Council," along with a "Chamber of Guardians" to enforce world law. Also included is a "Preamble" calling upon nations to surrender their arms to the world government, and including the right of this "Federal Republic of the World" to seize private property for its own use. Adler in the future will author *Haves Without Have-Nots* (1991), mentioning "vision" and describing the contributions of Marx and Lenin to our future.[19] He will assert that there will be a redistribution of wealth from the "have" to the "have-not" nations, professing that "this can be done only by the regulations of a world economy by a world government." He will further say that all participating nations must be "socialist" and surrender "every vestige of national sovereignty in dealing with one another." World government would preclude nations' "foreign policies, military installations and personnel, and immigration barriers," and the U.S.A. and its NATO allies along with the U.S.S.R. and its Warsaw Pact allies would be replaced by the USDR (Union of Socialist Democratic Republics), according to Adler.

▪ F. O. Matthiessen (Rhodes Scholar 1923 and pacifist and socialist) is waiting to testify to the U.S. House Committee on Un-American Activities, and dines at the apartment of Donald Ogden Stewart. Eileen Finletter is also at the dinner, and recalled later: "I very distinctly heard Matty say to Don Stewart, 'As long as we have somebody from Bones who can bring pressure on the committee, I think we'll be all right.'" "Bones" refers to the Yale University "Skull and Bones" society, of which future President George Bush would be a member in this same year of 1948.

▪ *International Government* by Clyde Eagleton (Rhodes Scholar 1914) is published. In this second edition (the first edition was published in 1932), he proclaims:

> I am concerned with . . . the slowly evolving constitutional law and organization of the community of nations, developing toward international, or world, government. . . . The following arguments have been offered in favor of regionalism: (1) Development should

> be attempted gradually, rather than in one jump toward world government. Such a world system could be better built upon the solid foundation of regional systems. . . .

▪ *UNESCO: Its Purpose and Its Philosophy* by Sir Julian Huxley (Fabian Socialist and the first director-general of UNESCO, 1946–48) is published, in which he proclaims:

> The general philosophy of UNESCO should be a scientific world humanism, global in extent and evolutionary in background. . . . In its education program it can stress the ultimate need for world political unity and familiarize all peoples with the implications of the transfer of full sovereignty from separate nations to a world organization. . . . Political unification in some sort of world government will be required. . . . Tasks for the media division of UNESCO [will be] to promote the growth of a common outlook shared by all nations and cultures . . . to help the emergence of a single world culture. . . . Even though it is quite true that any radical eugenic policy will be for many years politically and psychologically impossible, it will be important for UNESCO to see that the eugenic problem is examined with the greatest care, and that the public mind is informed of the issues at stake so that much that now is unthinkable may at least become thinkable.

1949

▪ April: *United Nations World* magazine publishes an article by Ambassador Warren Austin, chief of the U.S. Mission to the U.N., in which he pronounces that

> . . . all of us today need . . . the far vision in world affairs. . . . We must look far ahead to our final goal of world peace under law: that introduces World Federation. . . . World government could not be accepted without radical change of national outlook. . . . It will take a long time to prepare peoples and governments of most nations for acceptance of and participation in a world government. . . . If we expect this future world government to be created by agreement and not by force or conquest, we will have to be willing to work patiently until peoples or governments are ready for it. . . .

▪ *Towards World Understanding,* vol. V, is published by UNESCO, and in this volume one reads:

> As long as the child breathes the poisoned air of nationalism, education in world-mindedness can produce only rather precarious results. . . . For the moment, it is sufficient to note that it is most frequently in the family that the children are infected with nationalism by hearing what is national extolled and what is foreign disparaged. . . . The activity of the school cannot bring about the desired result unless, repudiating every form of nationalism. . . .

▪ The manuscript of *The Anglo-American Establishment* by Prof. Carroll Quigley is written, but he cannot find a publisher, and it is published posthumously in 1981. In this volume, he relates that The Group was trying

> to prevent influential people from using the League (of Nations) as an instrument of world government before popular opinion was ready for a world government. . . . When the influence which the RIIA wields is combined with that controlled by the Milner Group (The Group) in other fields—in education, in administration, in newspapers, and periodicals—a really terrifying picture begins to emerge. . . . The picture is terrifying because such power, whatever the goals at which it may be directed, is too much to be entrusted safely to any group. . . . No country that values its safety should allow what the Milner Group accomplished in Britain—that is, that a small number of men should be able to wield such power in administration and politics, should be given almost complete control over the publication of documents relating to their actions, should be able to exercise such influence over the avenues of information that create public opinion, and should be able to monopolize so completely the writing and teaching of the history of their own period.[20]

- *The World Must Be Governed* by Vernon Nash (Rhodes Scholar 1916) is published, in which the author comments:

> Among the prominent personnel who have been active in the previous World Federalists . . . [was] Edgar Ansel Mowrer, whose syndicated newspaper articles and personal contacts with American officials and with representatives of other countries in Washington and

> at Lake Success have advanced the cause effectively throughout the world.

Mowrer will also be with the League for Industrial Democracy (formerly the Intercollegiate Socialist Society), the Americans for Democratic Action, and on the board of the U.S. Committee for the Atlantic Congress (pursuing a union of the U.S. with other countries). He will, like Stanley Hornbeck (Rhodes Scholar 1904), be on the 1964 listing of the American Security Council's Cold War advisory committee. At the beginning of the book, Nash emphasizes transforming "vision" into reality, and chapter titles include "The U.N. Merely Camouflages Power Politics" and "One Option: World Government or Cataclysm." Nash is vice-president of United World Federalists.

▪ July 26: Eighteen members of the U.S. Senate sponsor Senate Concurrent Resolution 56 calling for the U.N. to be developed into a world federation. Leading the senators is Senator Glen Taylor (D-Idaho), whose secretary is G. H. Curtis (Rhodes Scholar 1908), and the Resolution will be reintroduced February 9, 1950, as Senate Concurrent Resolution 66.

The Resolution begins: "Whereas, in order to achieve universal peace and justice, the present Charter of the United Nations should be changed to provide a true world government constitution." Senator Alexander Wiley (R-Wisconsin) calls it "a consummation devoutly to be wished for. . . . I understand [the] proposition is either change the United Nations, or change or create, by a separate convention, a world order." And Senator Taylor will later state: "We would have to sacrifice considerable sovereignty to the world organization to enable them to levy taxes in their own right to support themselves."

▪ *The New World Order* by communist Scott Nearing is published, in which he projects that "the one world of technology must become one world also economically and politically. . . . Such objectives will be achieved most easily through a science of social engineering."

▪ George Orwell's *1984* is published warning of a future under an authoritarian "Big Brother." When the character, Winston, in the book tells "Big Brother's" agent, O'Brien, that they will not be successful in their plans to control people's behavior, O'Brien replies: "Suppose that we quicken the tempo of human life. . . ." One should keep in mind the ever-quickening tempo of life since the 1940s and the hyper-reality today of certain types of music and television commercials. Also, if one is kept very busy performing many tasks each day, there is less time for individuals to reflect upon societal or other forces causing problems and to organize in opposition to them.

Just as Robert Hugh Benson in *Lord of the World* in 1907 wrote of things that would happen at the end of this century, Lewis Carroll (member of the Society for Psychical Research) foreshadowed what O'Brien alluded to in Orwell's *1984.* In Carroll's *Alice's Adventures in Wonderland* (1865), the white rabbit is frantically running around, worrying that he'll be too late. In Carroll's

Through the Looking Glass (1872), Alice exclaims: "It's a great huge game of chess that's being played—all over the world." Alice then says she "wouldn't mind being a Pawn," and she starts running with the Queen, who says: "Faster! Faster!" When they stopped, they were still under the same tree, and the Queen said: "It takes all the running *you* can do, to keep in the same place. If you want to get somewhere else, you must run at least twice as fast as that." (Also see entry for September 11, 1998.)

1950

▪ Dennis Stanfill becomes a Rhodes Scholar and will later become chairman and CEO of Twentieth-Century Fox as well as chairman of Metro-Goldwyn-Mayer.

▪ September–October: The Foreign Policy Association "Headline Series" number 83, "Which Way to World Government?" by Alfred Lilienthal is published, in which he writes: "At Montreaux the formation of regional federations, in so far as they did not become an end in themselves, was favorably regarded as a step toward the effective functioning of world government." Lilienthal had worked for the State Department and was a consultant to the U.S. delegation to the U.N. conference in San Francisco in 1945.

▪ October: The *American Oxonian* publishes a list of twenty prominent Rhodes Scholars in government, including Carl Albert (Rhodes Scholar 1931) from Oklahoma, who will become Speaker of the U.S. House of Representatives.

▪ October 24: President Truman proclaims:

> The United Nations represents the idea of a universal morality, superior to the interests of individual nations. . . . The men who laid down their lives for the United Nations in Korea. . . . They died in order that the United Nations might live.

1951

▪ July 15: On the front page of the *Chicago Tribune* is an article concerning Cecil Rhodes' goal, and it states:

> Today many American Rhodes scholars are working assiduously to make the dream of their imperial patron come true. . . . More than a third of the 1,185 living American scholars are in the educational field. . . . Rhodes scholars also command posts in the United Nations and economic cooperation administration. The returning savants are active in the field of opinion molding with a large sprinkling among the eastern internationalist press, magazines, and radio.

▪ July 21: The *Chicago Tribune* publishes a front page article titled "Rhodes' Wards Head Global Foundations: Dole Out Cash for One Worlders." It describes funding by the Carnegie Foundation for the Advancement of Teaching headed by O. C. Carmichael (Rhodes Scholar 1913), and by the Carnegie Endowment for International Peace whose president has been Alger Hiss (now in a federal prison for perjury involving wartime espionage for the Russians). It also describes funding by the Rockefeller Foundation with Rhodes Scholars such as A. W. Packard, E. F. D'Arms, Chadbourne Gilpatric, J. L. Hydrick, D. P. C. Lloyd, Henry Allen Moe, Dean Clark, and Dean Rusk (as a member of the board of trustees).

▪ July 22: *Chicago Tribune* staff writer William Fulton notes that

> the American Rhodes Scholars network in the United States—is completed and glued together by their numbers in the field of molding public opinion. . . . Rhodes Scholars in the public opinion field constitute a faithful clique for their colleagues in the government, primarily in the State Department which they dominate. . . . With this tie-in, they're attempting to bring about the fulfillment of the lifelong ambitions held by their educational benefactor, Cecil John Rhodes.

One of the officers at the State Department at this time is S. Shepard Jones (Rhodes Scholar 1933), who will be one of the professors (along with a former CIA covert agent) who will teach political science courses to the writer of this chronology while a doctoral student at UNC-Chapel Hill in the early 1970s. Other Rhodes Scholars at the State Department at this time are James Fowler and D. M. French (both in the Bureau of United Nations Affairs), and Rhodes Scholars at the U.N. itself include Walter Chudson, Marshall Wolfe, S. M. Keeny, C. B. Wicart, and Charles Bolte.

Concerning the press, magazines, and media, the *Tribune* article lists the following prominent RS: Samuel

Welles, C. T. Solberg, and H. B. Hering with *Time;* Hedley Donovan with *Fortune;* Ernest Lindley with *Newsweek;* Beverly Smith with the *Saturday Evening Post;* H. L. Brown, Jr., with *Kiplinger Magazine;* Thomas J. Hamilton, Jr., Clarence Streit, Robert Aura Smith, John Oakes, and W. F. Fowle with *The New York Times;* William Nichols, J. M. Minifie, and R. W. Dunlap with *The New York Herald Tribune;* E. D. Canham and Donovan Richardson with *The Christian Science Monitor;* R. P. Brandt with *The St. Louis Post-Dispatch;* F. W. Beirne with *The Baltimore Sun;* Elmer Davis with the *American Broadcasting Company* (ABC); and Howard K. Smith and Charles Collingwood with the *Columbia Broadcasting System* (CBS). In addition, C. J. Durr was a commissioner with the Federal Communications Commission; John Fischer was editor of *Harpers* magazine; G. A. Gordon, Jr., was managing editor of *Good Housekeeping;* Robert Lasch was an editorial writer for *The Chicago Sun;* Harlan Logan was editor of *Look* magazine; Frank Morley (one of the founders of the socialist Oxford Labour Club) was editor of Harcourt, Brace and Co.; R. H. Peters was managing editor of *The Seattle Post–Intelligencer;* A. E. Rollins was managing editor of *Compton's Encyclopedia;* and Joseph Brandt was president of Henry Holt and Co. publishing.[21]

▪ Herman Dinsmore becomes foreign editor of *The New York Times,* and will remain in that position until 1960. In his book, *All the News That Fits* (1969), he will write:

> *The New York Times* today is deliberately pitched to the so-called liberal point of view. . . . Positively and negatively, the weight of *The [New York] Times* has gener-

ally fallen on the side of the communists since the end of World War II.

▪ July 23: *The Chicago Tribune* publishes an article, "Canada Offers Fine Field to Rhodes' Wards," in which is stated:

> When Gen. MacArthur displeased Britain and Canada by his efforts to win the Korean War, Canada's Oxford educated minister for external affairs, Lester B. Pearson, complained that American-Canadian relations had become "difficult and delicate." MacArthur was fired the next day. Pearson's foreign office staff is packed with Rhodes scholars.

Canadian Prime Minister Lester Pearson will be a First Endorser of Planetary Citizens.

▪ July 24: *The Chicago Tribune* publishes a front page news article titled "'Global' Flag Gen. Ike's Aim, Says Senator," which begins with the words: "Gen. Eisenhower is working for an allied army under a single flag, uniform, and command to defend Western Europe, senators reported today on their return from an overseas inspection trip."

▪ July 31: *The Chicago Tribune* publishes an article, "OWI Propaganda Machine Linked to Rhodes Men," stating:

> Those who absorbed the [Elmer] Davis [Rhodes Scholar and head of OWI, Office of War Information] training have pushed the British concept of policing the world with American soldiers and economic aid

> and have fought for a world federation under which the United States would surrender its sovereignty.

About forty years later, American soldiers will be stationed in South Korea, Bosnia, and many other nations around the world as part of U.N. "peacekeeping missions."

▪ September: The World Association of Parliamentarians for World Government (WAPWG) is founded. Louis Sohn will be an American legal consultant to the organization, and he will co-author *World Peace Through World Law* (1958) with Grenville Clark. At WAPWG's 1952 London meeting, it will adopt a map describing what nations' forces will be policing what other nations when world government is achieved. The map will show that American forces will be in Yugoslavia (where they are today), in Australia (where they are today), and in Kazak SSR (on September 14, 1997, U.S. troops will begin a joint exercise in Kazakhstan). The same map will show Russian soldiers policing in Oklahoma (just south of Kansas) southward and eastward in the U.S. In October 1995, Russian soldiers will be at Ft. Riley, Kansas, in an exercise designed "to foster interoperability between U.S. and Russian soldiers." Similarly, former Soviet bloc countries' soldiers will be in exercises at Ft. Polk, Louisiana, in August 1997. And Russian police will be in southern towns like Beaumont, Mississippi (see *The Beaumont*, November 9, 1994), with one Russian officer even assisting in the arrest of three people in western North Carolina (see *The Lincoln Gazette*, March

12, 1995). The 1952 WAPWG map will also show Mongolians (Chinese) policing near Long Beach, California, where in the late 1990s the Communist Chinese via the China Ocean Shipping Company (COSCO) will be provided by the Clinton administration with a dedicated shipping terminal at the port of Long Beach.

Relevant here also is the fact that on May 11, 1991, *The Dallas Morning News* (and other newspapers around the nation) will report that "German lawmakers and U.S. officials reacted favorably to the idea of a permanent German military presence" in the U.S.

1952

▪ April 11: John Foster Dulles (who will become Secretary of State) in a speech before the American Bar Association in Louisville, Kentucky, states:

> Treaty law can override the Constitution. . . . Treaties can take powers away from Congress and give them to the President. They can take powers from the States and give them to the Federal Government or to some international body, and they can cut across the rights given to the people by their constitutional Bill of Rights.

1953

▪ Frank Wells becomes a Rhodes Scholar, and will later be president of Warner Brothers in Hollywood, and then president and chief operating officer of the Disney Corporation.

▪ *The Impact of Science on Society* by Fabian Socialist Bertrand Russell is published, in which he declares:

> I think the subject which will be of most importance politically is mass psychology. . . . Various results will soon be arrived at: that the influence of home is obstructive. . . . Although this science will be diligently studied, it will be rigidly confined to the governing class. The populace will not be allowed to know how its convictions were generated. When the technique has been perfected, every government that has been in charge of education for a generation will be able to control its subjects securely without the need of armies or policemen. . . . Educational propaganda, with government help, could achieve this result in a generation. There are, however, two powerful forces opposed to such a policy: one is religion; the other is nationalism. . . . A scientific world society cannot be stable unless there is a world government.

1954

▪ April 5: Rene Wormser, general counsel for the U.S. House of Representatives Special Committee to Investigate Tax-Exempt Foundations, writes to former Assistant Secretary of State and ambassador Spruille Braden concerning the Rhodes Scholarship Trust (and the Carnegie Endowment, Rockefeller Foundation, and Ford Foundation). On April 10, Braden will reply in writing:

> I have the very definite feeling that these various foundations you mention very definitely do exercise both

overt and covert influences on our foreign relations and that their influences are counter to the fundamental principles on which this nation was founded and which have made it great.

- May: The first meeting of the Bilderbergers is held at the Hotel Bilderberger in Oosterbeek, Holland. The meetings of these international elitists, including Rhodes Scholar Dean Rusk among others, will be held in secret. Prince Bernhard of Holland is the first chairman, and John J. McCloy will become a member of the steering committee.

- Don K. Price (Rhodes Scholar 1932–35) becomes vice-president of the Ford Foundation. He will remain in that position until 1958. From 1949 to 1952 he was director of the Social Science Research Council, a position he will also hold from 1964 to 1969. From 1961 to 1971 he will be a trustee of the Rand Corporation. And in 1983 he will author *America's Unwritten Constitution*.

- Paul Sarbanes becomes a Rhodes Scholar, and will enter the U.S. Senate in 1977.

- Richard Lugar becomes a Rhodes Scholar.[22]

- John Brademus receives his Ph.D. as a Rhodes Scholar. He will be a congressman from 1959 to 1981. He will be a CFR member and Trilateralist, and he will become chairman of the board of directors of the Rockefeller Foundation and the Aspen Institute for Humanistic Studies. He will be president of New York University from 1981 to 1992. And he will be a member of the Federal Reserve, a trustee of the Committee for Economic Development (CED), and a member of the Central Committee of the World Council of Churches.

1955

▪ July 9: *National* magazine publishes an article, "Our Outmoded Loyalties," by Brock Chisholm (a close friend of Alger Hiss and the first head of the World Health Organization), in which he advocates a blitzkrieg against The Past—against all "the ways of our ancestors [including] our constitutions . . . our economic and social structures. . . ." In the February 1946 edition of *Psychiatry*, he had already called for world government and for children to become world citizens, and had stated:

> We have swallowed all manner of poisonous certainties fed us by our parents, our Sunday and day school teachers, our politicians, our priests. . . . The reinterpretation and eventual eradication of the concept of right and wrong which has been the basis of child training, the substitution of intelligent and rational thinking for faith in the certainties of old people, these are the belated objectives . . . for charting the changes in human behavior.

1956

▪ *The Power Elite* by C. Wright Mills is published. He is a leftist Columbia University sociologist, and in his book, he acknowledges:

> There is . . . little doubt that the American power elite—which contains, we are told, some of "the greatest organizers in the world"—has . . . planned and plotted. . . . Certain types of men from each of the dominant institutional areas, more far-sighted than others, have actually promoted the liaison [of the power elite] before it took its truly modern shape. . . . The power elite is not altogether "surfaced." . . . Many higher events that would reveal the working of the power elite can be withheld from public knowledge under the guise of secrecy. With the wide secrecy covering their operations and decisions, the power elite can mark their intentions, operations and further consolidation. . . . New men come into it [the power elite] and assume its existence without question.

1958

- February 21: In the *Congressional Record* (p. 2560), Senator George W. Malone states:

> A great editor, Mr. E. F. Tompkins, of the *New York Journal-American,* has written five important articles regarding the relationship between free trade, free immigration, and world government. . . . In a letter addressed to me, Mr. Tompkins stated: "The free-trade movement is not a separate entity. It is related in this country to the opposition to immigration regulations, and both by adoption or devolution are parts of the world government movement." . . . On June 28, 1952, I said on the Senate floor—and my remarks were reprinted under the title "Free Economic System Versus

> Fabian Socialistic Program": "The international socialism plan calls for (a) Reduction of all barriers to the flow of international trade, (b) Access to raw materials of all sorts for all nations, (c) Access to markets for all nations, (d) A world organization through which the nations can share freely in the supplies and the markets of the world. There can be only one result and only one final solution if these objectives are allowed to obtain, and that is, of course, the leveling of the living standards of the United States of America with the sweatshop-labor nations of the world."

▪ Clarence Streit (Rhodes Scholar 1918) creates the International Movement for Atlantic Union.

▪ May 28: Attorney and radio commentator Sid Hardin writes a letter concerning H. N. Mallon, who was a member of Skull and Bones the same year (1917) as was Prescott Sheldon Bush (the father of George Bush, a member of Skull and Bones). Henry Neil Mallon of Dresser Industries (which helped build up the Soviet Union) helped the future President Bush get a job in the oil business. Hardin in his letter states:

> Confidentially, H. N. Mallon is under intensive investigation by the U.S. Naval Intelligence, Washington, D.C. Only recently a U.S. Naval Intelligence Officer called on me and photostatted my file on Mallon and Dresser Industries and questioned me for two hours and I was unable to answer his questions but obviously Mallon was suspected of some subversive ac-

> tivities or dealings with Russia, and the questions ran all the way from questions about cartels to connections with the Cuban revolt, activities in Venezuela, as well as Soviet Espionage Agents. He took my letter from Mallon criticizing my KRLD radio program, but returned it later. There is no doubt about it, Mallon is a dangerous operator.

- July: *Harper's Magazine* publishes "School for Statesmen" by national columnist Joseph Kraft concerning the importance of the Council on Foreign Relations (CFR). In this article, he reveals that

> the Council plays a special part in helping to bridge the gap between the two (political) parties, affording unofficially a measure of continuity when the guard changes in Washington. . . . In theory at least, the Council comes close to being an organ of what C. Wright Mills has called the Power Elite—a group of men, similar in interest and outlook, shaping events from invulnerable positions behind the scenes. . . . It has been called "the government in exile."

1959

- *The West in Crisis* by James Warburg is published, in which he proclaims that

> a world order without world law is an anachronism. . . . A world which fails to establish the rule of law over the nation–states cannot long continue to exist. We are living in a perilous period of transition from the era

> of the fully sovereign nation–state to the era of world government.

James Warburg is a CFR member and a founder of United World Federalists. He is also the son of Paul Warburg, an architect of the Federal Reserve.

▪ A. B. Dick Howard becomes a Rhodes Scholar and will later become a constitutional expert at the University of Virginia Law School. In the late 1980s and early 1990s he will help to write the new constitutions for Albania, Bulgaria, the Czech Republic, Hungary, Poland, and Rumania.

▪ *The Ugly American* is written by Eugene Burdick (Rhodes Scholar 1948) with William Lederer.

▪ September 29: At a symposium titled "The Future of Man," sponsored by Joseph E. Seagrams & Sons, Inc., Fabian Socialist Bertrand Russell asserts that

> in almost all civilized countries at present the school child salutes the national flag. He ought instead to salute the flag of the United Nations. He ought to salute some international symbol and not a national symbol.

In a September 12, 1933, letter to H. G. Wells, Russell had written that his (Russell's) Beacon Hill School was pursuing a "social synthesis, . . . and this is what our children are grappling with. We *are* the new planned society in miniature."

1960

▪ *The United States in the World Arena* by Walt Rostow (Rhodes Scholar 1936) is published. He is a CFR member who will become President John Kennedy's National Security Advisor, even though Otto Otepka (deputy director of the State Department's Office of Security) earlier refused to approve Rostow's security clearance. In this book, he declares:

> It is a legitimate American national objective to see removed from all nations—including the United States—the right to use substantial military force to pursue their own interest. Since this residual right is the root of national sovereignty and the basis for the existence of an international arena of power, it is, therefore, an American interest to see an end to nationhood as it has been historically defined.

▪ September 9: President Dwight Eisenhower signs Senate Joint Resolution 170 promoting the concept of a federal Atlantic Union.

1961

▪ September: State Department document number 7277, titled "Freedom From War: The U.S. Program for General and Complete Disarmament in a Peaceful World," is published while Dean Rusk (Rhodes Scholar 1931), CFR member, Bilderberger, and former president of the Rockefeller Foundation, is Secretary of State. The document details a three-stage plan, with one of its objectives "the disbanding of all national armed forces and the prohibition of their reestablishment in any form whatsoever other than those required to preserve internal order and for contributions to the United Nations Peace Force." A provision in the second stage is "the dismantling or the conversion to peaceful uses of certain military bases and facilities wherever located," which will fit the closing of many American military bases about thirty years later, with one of the most hallowed (in San Francisco) being taken over in April 1993 by the Gorbachev Foundation (named for Soviet leader Mikhail Gorbachev, who will say that his foundation at the former American military base is part of "The New World Order"). And according to the third stage of the document, progressive disarmament "would proceed to a point where no state would have the military power to challenge the progressively strengthened U.N. Peace Force."[23] Relevant federal public laws concerning arms control and disarmament will be P.L. 87-297 and P.L. 101-216.

In his September 25 address to the U.N. General Assembly, President Kennedy proclaims: "Let us join in dismantling the national capacity to wage war. . . . The program to be presented to this assembly [is] for general and complete disarmament." He calls for

> an international organization within the framework of the United Nations . . . (that) would achieve a steady reduction in force, both nuclear and conventional, until it had abolished all armies and all weapons except those needed for internal order and a new United Nations peace force. . . . The United States recom-

> mends that all member nations earmark special peace-keeping units in their armed forces—to be on call to the United Nations. . . .

In addition to Rusk and Rostow, President Kennedy brings ten other Rhodes Scholars into his administration (eventually there would be a total of about twenty-five), supposedly comprised of *"The Best and the Brightest,"* which will be the title of a book by David Halberstam, who writes therein:

> . . . Titles become particularly important. . . . To make it in America, to rise, there has to be some sort of propellant; sheer talent helps, but except in very rare instances, talent is not enough. Money helps, family ties and connections help; for someone without these the way to the power elite can seem too far, too hopeless to challenge. The connection is often a Rhodes scholarship. It is a booster shot that young men are not unaware of, that will make the rest of their lives a good deal easier. Doors will open more readily, invitations will arrive, the phone will ring.

Eleven years earlier, in March 1950, Rusk had been appointed an Assistant Secretary of State, taking the place of W. W. Butterworth (Rhodes Scholar 1924).

Also appointed under Kennedy are National Education Association member Elvis Stahr, Jr. (Rhodes Scholar 1936) as Secretary of the Army (he was president of West Virginia University and would later be president of Indiana University and president of the Audubon Society);

George McGhee (Rhodes Scholar 1934–37) as Undersecretary of State for Political Affairs; Alain Enthoven (Rhodes Scholar 1952) as Deputy Assistant Secretary of Defense; Harlan Cleveland (Rhodes Scholar 1938) as an Assistant Secretary of State; Charles Hitch (Rhodes Scholar 1932–33) as Assistant Secretary of Defense and comptroller (where he develops the controversial Planning-Programming-Budgeting System, PPBS), who will become president of the University of California; and CFR member, former OSS member, Keynesian (Fabian) economist, and Federal Reserve spokesman Robert Roosa (Rhodes Scholar 1939) as Undersecretary of the Treasury for Monetary Affairs and chief financial strategist for President Kennedy's "New Frontier." Upon leaving government, Roosa will go with Brown Brothers, Harriman and Co. [Averell Harriman was a member of the "Skull and Bones" society in 1913 as was his brother, E. R. Harriman, in 1917. Walter Brown was initiated in 1945, and partner Prescott Bush (George Bush's father) was initiated in 1917.]

1962

- January 16: *Look* magazine publishes Israeli Prime Minister David Ben-Gurion's prediction of what the world will look like in twenty-five years. He states:

> The image of the world in 1987 as traced in my imagination: The Cold War will be a thing of the past . . . a gradual democratization of the Soviet Union. . . . On the other hand, the United States [will be transformed] into a welfare state with a planned economy. Western

> and Eastern Europe will become a federation of autonomous states having a Socialist and democratic regime. With the exception of the U.S.S.R. as a federated Eurasian state, all other continents will become united in a world alliance, at whose disposal will be an international police force. . . . A pill to prevent pregnancy will slow down the explosive natural increase in China and India. . . .

▪ March 10: The Institute for Defense Analyses, under contract SCC 28270 with the State Department (headed by Rhodes Scholar Dean Rusk), presents Study Memorandum No. 7, "A World Effectively Controlled by the United Nations," written by CFR member Lincoln Bloomfield, in which he states:

> A world effectively controlled by the United Nations is one in which "world government" would come about through the establishment of supranational institutions, characterized by mandatory universal membership and some ability to employ physical force. . . . [But] if the communist dynamic was greatly abated, the West might lose whatever incentive it has for world government.

▪ March 31: *Los Angeles Times* midday headline, "U.S. Formula for Peace: One Military Force Under U.N. Control," and final edition headline, "U.S. to Propose End of National Armies."

▪ July 11: *The New York Times* publishes an article by CFR member James Reston on its editorial page concerning

President Kennedy's July 4th address calling for a "declaration of interdependence" (with federal institutions) between the U.S. and Europe. In this column, Reston states:

> Maybe it's just the drowsy indolence of the summertime, but American opinion seems remarkably receptive, or at least acquiescent, to President Kennedy's proposal for a "partnership" of the Atlantic nations. . . . This year, President Kennedy went to Independence Hall, of all places, and on the Fourth of July, of all days; and virtually proposed to repeal the Declaration of Independence in favor of a declaration of international interdependence. Yet very little happened, . . . here in Washington not a whisper of protest from a single national leader.

▪ *Theory of Collective Behavior* by Neil Smelser (Rhodes Scholar 1952) is published. He will be a trustee of the Center for Behavioral Sciences and the Russell Sage Foundation. And in 1996–97, he will be president of the American Sociological Association.

▪ "The Future of Federalism" is a series of lectures (published as a book in 1964) at Harvard University by Nelson Rockefeller (Governor of New York 1959–73), in which he claims that current events compellingly demand "a new world order," as the old order is crumbling, and there is

> a new and free order struggling to be born. . . . [There is a] fever of nationalism . . . [but] the nation–state is

> becoming less and less competent to perform its international political tasks. . . . These are some of the reasons pressing us to lead vigorously toward the true building of a new world order . . . [with] voluntary service. . . . Sooner perhaps than we may realize, . . . there will evolve the bases for a federal structure of the free world.

1963

- Robert W. Barnett (Rhodes Scholar 1934–37) becomes a Deputy Assistant Secretary of State and will remain in that position until 1970. He has earlier been a General Education board fellow and a Rockefeller Foundation fellow. He has also been a CFR member and a staff member of the leftist Institute of Pacific Relations. From 1979 to 1985 he will be a resident associate of the Carnegie Endowment for International Peace.

- September 30: President Kennedy (former CFR member) addresses a meeting of the International Monetary Fund, and states:

> Twenty years ago, when the architects of these institutions met to design an international banking structure, the economic life of the world was polarized in overwhelming, and even alarming measure, on the United States. So were the world's monetary reserves. . . . Sixty percent of the gold reserves of the world were here in the United States. . . . There was a need for redistribution of the financial resources of the world. . . . All this has come about. It did not come about by

> chance but by conscious and deliberate and responsible planning. . . . We are now entering upon a new era of economic and financial interdependence. . . . Our gold reserves are . . . (now) forty percent of the world's holdings.

▪ November 18: *U.S. News and World Report* writes that President Kennedy's new policy line (as stated in his June 10 and October 19 speeches) concerning Soviet-American relations is one of "togetherness" and "interdependence."

1964

▪ Bill Clinton graduates from high school and attends Georgetown University in Washington, D.C. Georgetown is run by Jesuits, one of whom is a priest, Avery Dulles (son of John Foster Dulles), and he will be on the university's Board of Directors from 1966–68, the last two years Bill Clinton attends there.

Bill Clinton's political mentor will be Senator J. William Fulbright of Arkansas (Rhodes Scholar 1925), who in this year authors *Old Myths and New Realities,* announcing: "Indeed, the concept of national sovereignty has become in our time a principle of international anarchy. . . . The sovereign nation can no longer serve as the ultimate unit of personal loyalty and responsibility." Bill Clinton will be Senator Fulbright's aide during Clinton's middle years at Georgetown.[24]

As an example of how the Hegelian dialectic works in terms of using or controlling both ends of an argument or issue, while Sen. Fulbright's views expressed in this book are similar to those of State Department document number 7277 released under fellow Rhodes Scholar Dean Rusk, the latter will take the "hawk" position concerning the Vietnam War while the former will push the anti-war "dove" position as chairman of the Senate Foreign Relations Committee. Bill Clinton will also protest the war. And in March 1994, a World Affairs Council chapter will give Dean Rusk its "World Citizen Award."

Earlier, at the same time George Mitchell (Rhodes Scholar 1926) and Haven Perkins (Rhodes Scholar 1923) were with the Congress of Industrial Organizations (CIO), G. O. Farmer (Rhodes Scholar 1936), E. K. McClaskey (Rhodes Scholar 1934) and Martin Wagner (Rhodes Scholar 1935) were with the National Labor Relations Board.

▪ James Gustave Speth becomes a Rhodes Scholar. He will be a law clerk to U.S. Supreme Court Justice Hugo Black, a co-founder of the Natural Resources Defense Council, and according to *National Review* (September 1, 1997) he's the "crafter of the doomladen Global 2000 report." He will be a senior presidential campaign advisor for Bill Clinton in 1992, and U.N. Secretary-General Boutros Boutros-Ghali will after that make him head of the United Nations Development Program (funds population control, such as Third World abortions).

▪ Larry Pressler (U.S. Senator from South Dakota, 1979–97) becomes a Rhodes Scholar.

1965

▪ Bill Bradley becomes a Rhodes Scholar, and in his *Life on the Run* (1976), he will write:

> At Oxford . . . I questioned my religious faith and sought workable moral values instead of simply rules. I became more playful and rebellious, responding to events in a way that discipline and obligation had outlawed before. . . . Specific studies were neglected without guilt. . . .

He will be a U.S. Senator from New Jersey from 1979 to 1996.

▪ Dr. Robert Ebert (Rhodes Scholar 1936–39) becomes dean of Harvard University's Medical School.

1966

▪ *Tragedy and Hope* by Prof. Carroll Quigley is published, in which he reveals that:

> There does exist, and has existed for a generation, an international . . . network which operates, to some extent, in the way the radical Right believes the Communists act. In fact, this network, which we may identify as the Round Table Groups, has no aversion to cooperating with the Communists, or any other groups, and frequently does so. I know of the operations of this network because I have studied it for twenty years and was permitted for two years, in the early 1960s, to examine its papers and secret records. I have no

> aversion to it or to most of its aims and have, for much of my life, been close to it and to many of its instruments. I have objected, both in the past and recently, to a few of its policies, . . . but in general my chief difference of opinion is that it wishes to remain unknown, and I believe its role in history is significant enough to be known.

▪ *The Merchant Bankers* by Joseph Wechsberg is published. Wechsberg is the son and grandson of merchant bankers. He was a technical sergeant in the psychological warfare division of the Czech army prior to joining the staff of *The New Yorker* magazine. On the back cover of this book about Rothschilds, Warburgs, Lehman Brothers, and others, it refers to "the secret fraternity" and "the world's most cloistered elite . . . whose family decisions have shaped the fates of kings and nations." Wechsberg quotes Lord Byron as saying, "Every loan . . . seats a Nation or upsets a Throne." Speaking of these financiers historically, Wechsberg explains that

> the merchant bankers . . . made enormous profits . . . and . . . organized a worldwide intelligence system and network of agents. . . . They knew the best kept secrets. . . . Today only government agencies could compile such vast files of economic information and political intelligence.

1967

▪ February 3: The American military newspaper *Stars and Stripes* prints a news item about Michael McGhee being arrested in California for "driving under the influence of LSD." The next day, the newspaper's editor, Col. George Moranda, will be relieved of his command and ordered to report back to the U.S. from the European armed forces news network where he is located. The news item is printed over the objections of Michael's father, George McGhee, U.S. ambassador to Germany. Ambassador McGhee, a Rhodes Scholar (1934–37) is located in Bonn where *The New York Times* bureau will file a dispatch of March 2 indicating that Ambassador McGhee telephoned "a ranking general at Army headquarters to bypass Moranda," whose superiors order him to pull the news item from remaining issues. Bureau Chief T. J. Hamilton (Rhodes Scholar 1928) had joined the *Times* staff in 1936 and became chief of the U.N. bureau, succeeding another Rhodes Scholar, Clarence Streit. In television, Charles Collingwood (Rhodes Scholar 1939) made U.N. broadcasts for CBS. It is not known to whom Ambassador McGhee appealed, but recent military personnel who have been Rhodes Scholars include Brig. Gen. William Connor (Chief of Staff G-3, Allied Land Forces in Central Europe), Herbert Bennington (a technical director with the Joint Chiefs of Staff at the Pentagon), Thomas Lynn Beyer (an analyst with the CIA who is now with the Department of Army), Lt. Gen. Charles Bonesteel III (with the office of Chief of Staff at the Pentagon), Charles Lister (with the Undersecretary of the Air Force), Col. Bernard Rogers (Office of the Chairman, Joint Chiefs of Staff), and the late John McNaughton who died before he could take the appointment as Secretary of the Navy. Ambassador

McGhee also said: "The Treaty of Rome (1957), which brought the Common Market into being, was nurtured at Bilderberg meetings."

▪ March 26: Pope Paul VI writes *Populorum Progressio* calling for "a new juridical order" and stating:

> Who can fail to see the need and importance of thus gradually coming to the establishment of a world authority capable of taking effective action on the juridical and political planes? . . . Delegates to international organizations, public officials, gentlemen of the press, teachers and educators—all of you must realize that you have your part to play in the construction of a new world order.

▪ July: Kermit Gordon (Rhodes Scholar 1938–39) becomes president of the Brookings Institution, after having been director of the federal budget under Presidents Kennedy and Johnson. On September 29, 1966, Johnson addresses dinner guests at the Brookings Institution saying it is "a national institution, so important to the executive branch and, I think, the Congress and the country." In a September 1967 article in *Social Science*, Brookings will be described as "Schoolmaster to the Government," with Kermit Gordon saying it "has one foot in the Government. We all know each other . . . the movement back and forth is increasing at high levels." Gordon is a Keynesian (Fabian) economist, trustee of the Ford Foundation and Committee for Economic Development (CED), and CFR member.

▪ October: In this edition of the CFR's *Foreign Affairs* is an article, "Asia After Vietnam," by Richard Nixon, in which he writes of nations' disposition "to evolve regional approaches to development needs and to the evolution of a new world order."

1968

▪ *The Subtle and Leisurely Penetration*, an adult education study and reference report from the George Mason School of Correspondence, is published by Education Information, Inc., of Sacramento, California. It mentions that the thirty-two Americans to be Rhodes Scholars this year have been selected, and then states: "The stated objectives of Cecil John Rhodes and his friend, Sir Andrew Carnegie, included the reduction of the United States to a colony of the New World Order."

▪ Bill Clinton graduates from Georgetown University. Prior to graduating, he will write to childhood friend Patty Criner: "You won't believe this, but the professors want me to apply [for a Rhodes scholarship]." Prof. Quigley had encouraged Clinton to apply for a Rhodes Scholarship, and had written a letter of recommendation on his behalf for it. Remember, this is *after* Prof. Quigley had looked at the power elite's "secret records," and after he had written *Tragedy and Hope* and *The Anglo-American Establishment*. Senator Fulbright had also recommended Clinton for a Rhodes Scholarship. And Clinton would later tell an interviewer, "That's one reason I wanted to try to get one [a Rhodes scholarship], because I knew Senator Fulbright had been one as well."

Bill Clinton is successful in his pursuit of a Rhodes Scholarship, and enters Oxford University this year, sometimes wearing a pink poplin suit. He also will help to organize two demonstrations against the Vietnam War outside the American Embassy in London. And he will later admit that while at Oxford (at twenty-two years of age), he experiments with marijuana "a time or two."

Another Rhodes Scholar (1958–60), famous singer and actor Kris Kristofferson, will also have trouble with drugs. He will later say his songwriting was "influenced in one way or another by the freedom I was exposed to at Oxford. It was at such a liberating time of my life." His albums "Jesus Was a Capricorn" and "Shake Hands with the Devil" will be released in 1972 and 1979 respectively. Also related to drugs, Kurt Schmote (Rhodes Scholar 1971, who will become mayor of Baltimore in 1988) will suggest that decriminalization of drugs could stop related crime and violence. There is much evidence to the contrary, and Schmote is severely criticized for his position.

A fellow Rhodes Scholar this year is Rick Stearns who will be a traveling companion with Bill Clinton, who after becoming president will appoint Stearns to the position of a U.S. District Court Judge in Massachusetts. Another Rhodes Scholar this year is Douglas Eakeley, whom President Clinton will appoint as chairman of the Legal Services Corporation.

▪ July 26: Presidential candidate, New York Governor Nelson Rockefeller, pledges that "as president, he would work toward international creation of a new world order," according to the Associated Press report.

▪ James Simon Kunen's *The Strawberry Statement* is published by Random House. In this book, Kunen tells of an SDS (Students for a Democratic Society) strategy meeting he attended where a student was giving a report about an SDS convention the student had recently attended. The student's report revealed that

> . . . men from Business International Roundtables . . . tried to buy up a few radicals. Those men are the world's industrialists and they convene to decide how our lives are going to go. They're the left wing of the ruling class. They offered to finance our demonstrations in Chicago. We were also offered ESSO [Rockefeller] money. They want us to make a lot of radical commotion so they can look more in the center as they move more to the left.

▪ U.S. Supreme Court Justice William O. Douglas in *Towards a Global Federalism* writes:

> Building bridges with Communist nations is the prime necessity of the day. . . . We have moved from free enterprise to a *sui generis* form of socialism. The trend toward the collective society will continue. . . . The Western and Soviet regimes may yet evolve into comparable economic systems. . . . The new [global] federalism would deal with conflicts between nations just as our own Supreme Court deals with conflicts between sovereign states.

1969

▪ *Nationalism and Its Alternative* by Karl Deutsch is published, in which this Harvard University professor warns about placing more authority in the hands of a single world system. He remarks:

> A (world) government that had all control in one centralized place for decision making about the enforcement of law would have control over the law, much as the Roman Legions had control over the Roman Empire. Once such a government controlled all laws, it would be able to control all aspects of life.

▪ December 2: U.S. Rep. George Bush introduces House Concurrent Resolution 460, which states in part:

> Whereas a joining together for such purposes of the democratic nations of the Atlantic community to create an Atlantic Union within the framework of the United Nations would reduce the cost of the common defense, provide a stable currency . . . , a declaration that the goal of their people is to transform their present alliance into a federal union.

1970

▪ January/February: *The Humanist* magazine publishes an article in which well-known CBS and ABC news commentator Howard K. Smith (Rhodes Scholar 1937) remarks:

> It is going to cause a wrench in sentiment and attitude, but we are going to have to adjust to limiting

> population. . . . We may even have to begin penalizing people by tax measures to induce them to do no more than have two children.

While at Oxford, Smith was elected president of the socialist Labour Club in 1939.

▪ *Between Two Ages: America's Role in the Technetronic Era* by Zbigniew Brzezinski is published. Brzezinski is a CFR member who will become the first director of the Trilateral Commission and President Carter's national security advisor. In this book, he states:

> Marxism represents a further vital and creative stage in the maturing of man's universal vision. Marxism is simultaneously a victory of the external, active man over the inner, passive man and a victory of reason over belief. . . . In the technetronic society the trend seems to be toward . . . effectively exploiting the latest communication techniques to manipulate emotions and control reason. . . . Human beings become increasingly manipulable and malleable. . . . The projected world information grid . . . could create the basis for a common educational program, for the adoption of common academic standards. . . . Today we are again witnessing the emergence of transnational elites . . . (whose) ties cut across national boundaries. . . . The nation-state is gradually yielding its sovereignty. . . . Further progress will require greater American sacrifices. More intensive efforts to shape a new world

monetary structure will have to be undertaken, with some consequent risk to the presently favorable American position.

1971

- March 26: "A Declaration of World Citizenship" is signed by Minnesota government officials, such as the governor and lieutenant governor, Senate and House majority and minority leaders, and others. The declaration proclaims: ". . . We pledge our efforts as world citizens to the

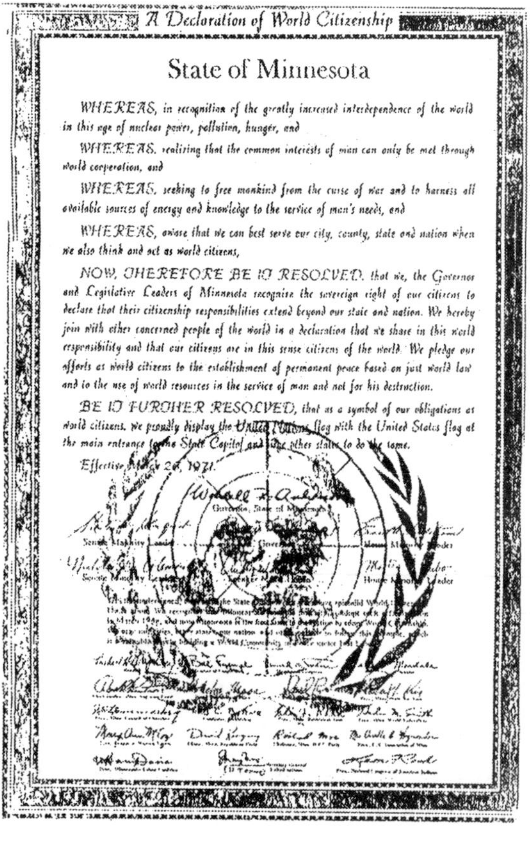
A Declaration of World Citizenship

State of Minnesota

WHEREAS, in recognition of the greatly increased interdependence of the world in this age of nuclear power, pollution, hunger, and

WHEREAS, realizing that the common interests of man can only be met through world corporation, and

WHEREAS, seeking to free mankind from the curse of war and to harness all available sources of energy and knowledge to the service of man's needs, and

WHEREAS, aware that we can best serve our city, county, state and nation when we also think and act as world citizens,

NOW, THEREFORE BE IT RESOLVED, that we, the Governor and Legislative Leaders of Minnesota recognize the sovereign right of our citizens to declare that their citizenship responsibilities extend beyond our state and nation. We hereby join with other concerned people of the world in a declaration that we share in this world responsibility and that our citizens are in this sense citizens of the world. We pledge our efforts as world citizens to the establishment of permanent peace based on just world law and to the use of world resources in the service of man and not for his destruction.

BE IT FURTHER RESOLVED, that as a symbol of our obligations as world citizens, we proudly display the United Nations flag with the United States flag at the main entrance to the State Capitol and urge other states to do the same.

Effective March 26, 1971.

Governor, State of Minnesota

establishment of permanent peace based on just world law. . . ."

▪ *Surviving the Future* by Arnold Toynbee (The Group) is published by Oxford University Press. In this book, the author proclaims:

> I expect that the World is going to be united politically in the teeth of nationalistic resistance. . . . The people of each local sovereign state will have to renounce their state's sovereignty and subordinate it to the paramount sovereignty of a literally world-wide world government. . . . I want to see a world government established.[25]

▪ September: *Psychology Today* publishes "Persuasion That Persists" by Milton Rokeach, who proclaims:

> Suppose you could take a group of people, give them a twenty-minute pencil-and-paper task, talk to them for ten to twenty minutes afterward, and thereby produce long-range changes in core values and personal behavior in a significant portion of this group. For openers, it would of course have major implications for education, government, propaganda, and therapy. . . . My colleagues and I have in the last five years achieved the kinds of results suggested in the first paragraph of this article. . . . It now seems to be within man's power to alter experimentally another person's basic values, and to control the direction of the change.

Five years earlier (1966), in another publication, Dr. James McConnell (professor of psychology at the University of Michigan) was similarly quoted as saying:

> I teach a course called The Psychology of Influence, and I begin it by stating categorically that the time has come when, if you give me any normal human being and a couple of weeks, . . . I can change his behavior from what it is not to whatever you want it to be, if it's physically possible. . . . I can turn him from a Christian into a communist and vice versa. . . . Look, we can do these things. We can control behavior.

1972

▪ May 18: Roy M. Ash, director of the Office of Management and Budget, declares that "within two decades the institutional framework for a world economic community will be in place . . . (and) aspects of individual sovereignty will be given over to a supernational authority."

▪ November 19: *The Los Angeles Times* publishes "A World Without Borders" by Lester Brown (CFR member), in which he states:

> Effective supranational institutions capable of coping with the technologies man has developed in fields ranging from nuclear weapons to weather modification invariably require that countries sacrifice a measure of sovereignty.

In 1974, Brown will found The Worldwatch Institute and

be its president, and the Institute will publish annual reports titled "State of the World." *The Washington Post* will describe Brown as "one of the world's most influential thinkers," and the Calcutta *Telegraph* will describe him as the "guru of the global environmental movement."

1973

- *The Coming of Post-Industrial Society* by noted sociologist Daniel Bell is published. Writing about the book in *The Futurist* (March-April 1996), David Snyder says it

> foresaw a society increasingly divided between a small, prosperous technocratic elite and a huge population of lower-middle-income service drones. From the very month it came out, the number of middle-class jobs as a share of *all* jobs in America fell, just as Bell had projected; it was almost as if he had programmed the economy.

- August 10: *The New York Times* publishes "From a China Traveller" by David Rockefeller, who writes:

> One is impressed immediately by the sense of national harmony. . . . There is a very real and pervasive dedication to Chairman Mao and Maoist principles. Whatever the price of the Chinese Revolution, it has obviously succeeded not only in producing more efficient and dedicated administration, but also in fostering high morale and community purpose. General social and economic progress is no less impressive. . . . The enormous social advances of China have benefitted

> greatly from the singleness of ideology and purpose. . . . The social experiment in China under Chairman Mao's leadership is one of the most important and successful in history.

According to Professor R. J. Rummel in *Death by Government*, at the time that Rockefeller is writing the above, the Communist Chinese regime is just completing the "termination" of 7.3 million units of "surplus human capital" in Chairman Mao's "glorious" Cultural Revolution.

▪ The Trilateral Commission is established by David Rockefeller.

▪ *The Second American Revolution* by John D. Rockefeller III is published, and it applauds sexual liberation and the "humanistic revolution," while disparaging "old-fashioned nationalism." The author was also the founder of the Population Council in 1952, and his father's cousin, Percy Rockefeller, was a member of Skull and Bones in 1900.

▪ The *Humanist Manifesto II* is released and states:

> Ethics is *autonomous* and *situational*. . . . We deplore the division of humankind on nationalistic grounds. . . . The best option is to *transcend the limits of national sovereignty*. . . . Thus we look to the development of a system of world law and a world order based upon transnational federal government.

1974

▪ April: Trilateralist and CFR member Richard Gardner's "The Hard Road to World Order" is published in the CFR's *Foreign Affairs*, and therein he states that

> the "house of world order" will have to be built from the bottom up rather than from the top down . . . but an end run around national sovereignty, eroding it piece by piece, will accomplish much more than the old-fashioned frontal assault.[26]

Gardner (Rhodes Scholar 1951–53) while Deputy Assistant Secretary of State authored *In Pursuit of World Order* (1964) with a foreword by Harlan Cleveland (Rhodes Scholar and CFR member). Gardner will be a member of the Consultation Planning Group for the Declaration of Interdependence in 1976, and he will then be appointed by President Jimmy Carter a few years later as Ambassador to Italy. In 1992, he will be an advisor to Bill Clinton during his presidential campaign, and later appointed by President Clinton as Ambassador to Spain, from which the new Secretary-General of NATO, Javier Solana, will come on December 5, 1995. Solana is a member of the Spanish Socialist Party, which in September 1979 will come to power saying, "We are a Marxist party," and which in the 1980s will try to close U.S. military bases in Spain. Solana will openly oppose Spain's membership in NATO, and he will express his admiration for Fidel Castro, who in October 1979 will address the U.N. General Assembly and demand a "new world order." The

Clinton administration will support Solana for the position of NATO Secretary-General.

▪ *Global Reach: The Power of the Multinational Corporations* by Richard J. Barnet and Ronald E. Müller is published, in which one reads:

> A company spokesman for Union Carbide [says]: "It is not proper for an international corporation to put the welfare of any country in which it does business above that of any other." . . . This vision stands as a direct challenge to traditional nationalism. Indeed, the world's leading corporate managers now see the nation-state . . . as the chief obstacle to planetary development. . . . Business International warns its corporate clients in a 1967 Research Report: ". . . the nation-state is becoming obsolete: tomorrow . . . it will in any meaningful sense be dead—and so will the corporation that remains essentially national."

Barnet is on the advisory board of the World Federalist Association, and he was a co-founder of the leftist Institute for Policy Studies.

▪ *Individual Rights and the Federal Role in Behavior Modification: Report of the Subcommittee on Constitutional Rights* is presented by the U.S. Senate Judiciary Committee, and in the preface one reads:

> Technology has begun to develop new methods of behavior control capable of altering not just an

> individual's actions but his very personality and manner of thinking as well. Because it affects the ability of the individual to think for himself, the behavioral technology being developed in the United States today touches upon the most basic sources of individuality, and the very core of personal freedom.

1975

- March 23: *The Washington Post* publishes an article about Prof. Carroll Quigley titled "The Professor Who Knew Too Much." Quigley will die less than two years later.

1976

- The *Declaration of Interdependence* is signed by a sizeable number of congressmen, including Les Aspin, a CFR member who has attended Oxford University. The document declares that "we must join with others to bring forth a new world order," and it decries "narrow notions of national sovereignty." It further calls upon all nations

> to strengthen and to sustain the United Nations . . . and to broaden the jurisdiction of the World Court, that these may preside over a reign of law that will not only end wars but end as well that mindless violence which terrorizes our society even in times of peace.

On July 8, 1977, Senator Jesse Helms will write that it is "a treasonable document." However, President Clinton will make Les Aspin his Secretary of Defense.

▪ General Bernard Rogers (Rhodes Scholar 1947) becomes Chief of Staff of the Army and remains in that position until 1979. He has also been on the board of directors of the Atlantic Council. From 1979 to 1987, he will be NATO's Supreme Allied Commander in Europe.

▪ The Aspen Institute for Humanistic Studies publishes "Interdependence Series No. 3," in which it states:

> The kind of educational transformation for which we have argued . . . will not come easily. Changing complex social institutions in any fundamental way requires unlimited quantities of sweat and almost certainly tears, if not blood.

The Freeman Digest (January 1979) will publish an interview with Joseph Slater, president of the Aspen Institute for Humanistic Studies, in which he will respond to the question about "the new world order" as follows:

> Whatever system is constructed, many people feel that the new global community will be monolithic; that is why the words "new world order" tend to connote a sort of *1984* Orwellian kind of notion where there is some master system. . . . There will be central direction on the basis of fairly diverse interaction. That is already taking place. Attitudes are being formed through that interaction rather than being imposed by somebody.

1977

▪ *Futures We Are In* by Fred Emery is published. Emery is

a senior staff member with the Tavistock Institute of Human Relations, and in this book is noted that he developed a theory of "social turbulence." According to this theory, many individuals faced with a series of crises will attempt to reduce the tension by adaptation and eventually psychological retreat. This then can lead to social disintegration. Could this be what America is experiencing today? Have many individuals, who earlier entered the struggle to preserve traditional values, been confronted with an emotional problem or crisis concerning schools, religion, politics, or some other area? Have they felt a strain or become weary of the battle, and decided either to adapt or give up the fight, rationalizing "What can one person do?"

▪ *The Third Try at World Order* by Harlan Cleveland (Rhodes Scholar 1938) is published. He is with the Aspen Institute for Humanistic Studies, a CFR member, and chairman of the U.S. Weather Modification Advisory Board, and in this book, he calls for "changing Americans' attitudes and institutions"; for "complete disarmament (except for international soldiers)"; for "fairer distribution of worldly goods through a new International Economic Order"; and for "international standards for individual entitlement to food, health and education." Cleveland's *Birth of a New World* will be published in 1993 with a foreword by Robert McNamara (CFR member and Trilateralist) saying, "Everybody is talking about 'a new world order.'" Cleveland along with three colleagues, including Lincoln Bloomfield, will organize something they will call "The Group" to come together to "rethink international governance," and that will serve as the basis for *Birth of a New World*.

In 1990, Cleveland will author *The Global Commons: Policy for the Planet*, published by the Aspen Institute for Humanistic Studies and by University Press of America, and containing a paper by Shirley Hufstedler (the first U.S. Secretary of Education, who also serves on the board of trustees for the Aspen Institute and the Carnegie Endowment for International Peace).

▪ July: *The Atlantic Monthly* publishes "The Trilateral Connection" by former *Washington Post* columnist Jeremiah Novak, in which he states:

> For the third time in this century, a group of American scholars, businessmen, and government officials is planning to fashion a New World Order. Discouraged by U.N. inadequacies, disheartened by chaos in the Bretton Woods institutions [International Monetary Fund and World Bank], and worried about the United States' waning strength, these men are looking to a "community of developed nations" to coordinate international political and economic affairs. . . . An overhauled IMF would provide another source of credit for [developing] nations, and would take the big private banks off the hook. This proposal is a cornerstone of the Trilateral plan. . . .

1979

▪ *With No Apologies* by former U.S. Senator Barry Goldwater is published, in which he explains:

> In my view the Trilateral Commission represents a skillful, coordinated effort to seize control and consolidate the four centers of power—political, monetary, intellectual, and ecclesiastical. All this is to be done in the interest of creating a more peaceful, more productive world community. What the Trilateralists truly intend is the creation of a worldwide economic power superior to the political governments of the nation-states involved. They believe the abundant materialism they propose to create will overwhelm existing differences. As managers and creators of the system they will rule the future.

1980

▪ *The Real War* by former President Nixon is published, in which he explains:

> The nation's immediate problem is that while the common man fights America's wars, the intellectual elite sets its agenda. Today, whether the West lives or dies is in the hands of its new power elite: those who set the terms of public debate, who manipulate the symbols, who decide whether nations or leaders will be depicted on 100 million television sets as "good" or "bad." This power elite sets the limits of the possible for Presidents and Congress. It molds the impressions that move the nation, or that mire it.

▪ *Fire in the Minds of Men* by James Billington is published. He is a Rhodes Scholar (1950–53) and CFR member who succeeds Daniel Boorstin (Rhodes Scholar 1934) as Librarian of Congress, and he says "this book seeks to trace the origins of a faith—perhaps *the* faith of our time.... What is new is the belief that a perfect secular order will emerge from the forcible overthrow of traditional authority." In this book, he describes mystic and spy Louis-Claude de Saint-Martin as "the high priest of mysticism (who) discovered in the mysterious chaos of revolution the possibility of building a new Jerusalem by means of Pythagorean forms and numbers." He goes on to describe how Buonarotti distilled his revolutionary plans from Babeuf, who was asked during the French Revolution to lead a "conspiracy of equals" establishing a communist society. He later describes the Utopianism of Robert Owen (who influenced John Ruskin, who in turn influenced Cecil Rhodes). The elitists' "revolutionary faith was shaped by occultism and proto-romanticism . . . and has become the most successful ideological export of the West to the world in the twentieth century," according to Billington.

- *Economic Democracy*, co-authored by Derek Shearer, is published. The book emphasizes a "vision," "change," a "new reality," and promotes what many understand to be a move toward socialism in America (e.g., national health care and insurance), and outlines a plan for a Democrat who would implement these policies to run for the presidency. Shearer will be associated with the leftist Institute for Policy Studies (IPS) and a friend and advisor to Bill Clinton, who as president will appoint a number of people associated with the IPS to positions in his administration.

▪ *Friendly Fascism: The New Face of Power in America* by Bertram Gross is published, and tells how computerized information could be used for "direct character assassination and defamation."

▪ *Charge It: Inside the Credit Card Conspiracy* by Terry Galanoy is published. He is former director of communications for National Bankamericard, later VISA, which lends credibility to his statement that

> George Orwell's notorious character "Big Brother" will actually turn out to be Big Banker; all-seeing, all-knowing, all-controlling, capable of destroying any resistance. . . . Where they're taking you is to a totally different kind of economic society in which you will have little or no privacy, in which your income and everything you own will be under their control. . . . You will be a profitable, dependable, fiscally sound, paid-up citizen even if they have to destroy your freedom and even your life to do it.

Relevant to Galanoy's reference to "Big Banker" as "all-seeing, all-knowing," and that "you will have little or no privacy," perhaps a first step in that direction will be taken when the Federal Reserve Board proposes that domestic and foreign banking organizations develop "Know Your Customer" programs. As proposed (posted in the *Federal Register,* December 1, 1998),

> the regulations would require each banking organization to develop a program designed to determine

> the true identity of its customers; determine its customers' sources of funds; determine, understand, and monitor the normal and expected transactions of its customers; and report appropriately any transactions of its customers that are determined to be unusual or suspicious. . . .

▪ *The Aquarian Conspiracy* by Marilyn Ferguson is published, in which she explains that

> there are legions of conspirators. . . . Of the Aquarian conspirators surveyed, more were involved in education than any other single category of work. . . . A major ambition of the curriculum is autonomy. This is based on the belief that if our children are to be free, they must be free even from us—from our limiting beliefs.

On July 23, 1982, future vice-president Al Gore will promote Ferguson's book, calling it "a focal point for what thousands of people with different backgrounds have been experiencing."

1981

▪ *Democratic Dictatorship: The Emergent Constitution of Control* by Arthur S. Miller is published, in which he describes a "new feudal order" controlled by elitists, and he asserts that "dictatorship will come—is coming—but with the acquiescence of the people. . . . The goal is 'predictable' man."

▪ September–October: *The Humanist* publishes an article by H. J. Blackham, a founder of the four million–member International Humanist and Ethical Union. In this article, Blackham remarks that if schools teach dependence (e.g., moral) on one's self, "they are more revolutionary than any conspiracy to overthrow the government."

▪ November 14: *The Nation* publishes an article in which American feminist activist Ellen Willis writes that

> feminism is not just an issue or a group of issues; it is the cutting edge of a revolution in cultural and moral values. . . . The objective of every feminist reform, from legal abortion to the E.R.A. to child-care programs, is to undermine traditional family values. . . .

1982

▪ John W. Sears (Rhodes Scholar 1955) becomes a candidate for the Office of Governor of Massachusetts. He was the registered representative of Brown, Brothers, Harriman & Co. from 1959 to 1965.

▪ *Minding America's Business* by Rhodes Scholars Ira Magaziner and Robert Reich is published. Magaziner has been earning up to six hundred dollars per hour advising companies like Corning and General Electric, and countries like Australia, Ireland, Israel, and Sweden.

1983

▪ Lois Quam becomes a Rhodes Scholar. She will later

become Minnesota's health commissioner and serve as a member of the Clinton health-care task force.

▪ *The Conservators* by FDR's son Elliott Roosevelt is published, in which he reveals that

> there are within our world perhaps only a dozen organizations which shape the courses of our various destinies as rigidly as the regularly constituted governments . . . this unofficial council of the elite, the creme de la creme of global planners.

1984

▪ *The Power to Lead* by James MacGregor Burns is published. Burns is a university professor who has been a member of the ACLU and ADA (Americans for Democratic Action), president of the International Society for Political Psychology, and who has done post-graduate work at the London School of Economics. In this book, he proclaims:

> Let us face reality. The framers [of the Constitution] have simply been too shrewd for us. They designed separate institutions that cannot be unified by mechanical linkages, frail bridges, tinkering. If we are to "turn the founders upside down" we must directly confront the constitutional structure they erected. . . . Others might press for major constitutional restructuring but I doubt that Americans under normal conditions could agree on the package of radical and "alien" constitutional changes that would be

required. They would do so, I think, only during and following a stupendous national crisis and political failure.

- November 11: Donald Keys delivers an address, "Transformation of Self and Society," at a symposium, "Toward a Global Society," in which he states:

> We're at a stage now of pulling it all together. It's a new religion called "networking." . . . When it comes to running a world or taking people into a New Age, . . . don't anyone think for a moment that you can run a planet without a head. . . . This planet has to be managed. . . . We have meditations at the United Nations a couple of times a week. The meditation leader is Sri Chinmoy, and this is what he said about this situation: ". . . The United Nations is the chosen instrument of God; to be a chosen instrument means to be a divine messenger carrying the banner of God's inner vision and outer manifestation. One day, the world will . . . treasure and cherish the soul of the United Nations as its very own with enormous pride, for this soul is all-loving, all-nourishing, and all-fulfilling."

Many trends at the U.N. have been started by Donald Keys, who has been a speechwriter for foreign ministers and ambassadors, and who is a founder of Planetary Citizens, along with Norman Cousins and former U.N. Secretary–General U Thant. First Endorsers of Planetary Citizens have included Arnold Toynbee, U.S. Supreme Court

Chief Justice Earl Warren, Robert Hutchins, Coretta Scott King, Linus Pauling, and Aurelio Peccei (founder of the Club of Rome). And on Planetary Citizens' advisory council have been Isaac Asimov, former U.N. Assistant Secretary–General Robert Muller, and Father Theodore Hesburgh (president of the University of Notre Dame), among others.

1985

▪ Carlton Stoiber (Rhodes Scholar 1964) becomes Counselor to the U.S. Mission to U.N. Agencies in Vienna, and occupies that position until 1988. He worked as an attorney in the U.S. Justice Department from 1969 to 1971, and he worked for the U.S. Arms Control and Disarmament Agency from 1980 to 1981.

▪ Andrew Nussbaum becomes a Rhodes Scholar and will later be a law clerk for future U.S. Supreme Court Justice Ruth Bader Ginsburg at the U.S. Court of Appeals in Washington, D.C., and then for U.S. Supreme Court Justice Antonin Scalia. He is the son of Bernard Nussbaum, who will be White House Counsel for President Clinton.

▪ The Carnegie Forum on Education and the Economy is established and in 1988 will change its name to the National Center on Education and the Economy. On its board will be Hillary Rodham Clinton, who will also serve on a Rhodes Scholarship selection committee.

1986

▪ *National Service: What Would It Mean?* is authored by Richard Danzig (Rhodes Scholar 1965). Danzig has been a law clerk for U.S. Supreme Court Justice Byron White and a Rockefeller Foundation Fellow. He will be a consultant to the U.N. Ctr. Transnational Corporation, and he will become Undersecretary of the Navy in 1993.

- August 16: In the Tax Reform Act of 1986, one finds that the new tax law applies to nearly everyone *except*

> any controlled foreign corporation which on August 16, 1986, was a member of an affiliated group as defined in section 1504 (a) of the Internal Revenue Code of 1986 without regard to subsection (b)(3) thereof, which had as its common parent a corporation incorporated in Delaware on July 9, 1967, with executive offices in New York, New York. . . .

Uncoincidentally, the American International Group (AIG) was incorporated in Delaware on July 9, 1967, with executive offices in New York, New York. This is an example of how the power elite can operate. Maurice Greenberg is CEO of AIG, and he is also a Trilateralist and CFR member. Henry Kissinger is on AIG's international advisory board. Greenberg also happens to be chairman of the Federal Reserve of New York, and on the February 19, 1997, "Charlie Rose Show" on PBS, future Assistant Secretary of State Richard Holbrooke (managing director of Lehman Brothers international bankers) will say that Greenberg probably knows the new leaders of communist China better than do the people in the U.S. government.

1987

▪ *The Secret Constitution and the Need for Constitutional Change* by Arthur S. Miller is published. In this book, sponsored in part by the Rockefeller Foundation, Miller asserts that

> . . . a pervasive system of thought control exists in the United States. . . . The citizenry is indoctrinated by employment of the mass media and the system of public education. . . . People are told what to think *about*. . . . The old order is crumbling. . . . Nationalism should be seen as a dangerous social disease. . . . A new vision is required to plan and manage the future, a global vision that will transcend national boundaries and eliminate the poison of nationalistic "solutions." . . . A new Constitution is necessary. . . . Americans really have no choice, for constitutional alteration will come whether or not it is liked or planned for. . . . Ours is the age of the planned society. . . . No other way is possible.

1987–1988

▪ Fall 1987/Spring 1988: *Breakthrough,* the quarterly publication of Global Education Associates, publishes an article, "The Rise of INGOs: New Leadership for a Planet in Transition," by sociologist Elise Boulding, one of the first endorsers of Planetary Citizens. In the Introduction to the article, one reads that "the proliferation of INGOs [international non-governmental organizations] shows how far the international system has already moved beyond the nation-state level." INGOs have sections in all member states of the U.N.

1988

▪ September 29: Ted Koppel (CFR member) on ABC's "Nightline" refers to nationalism as a "virus."

▪ November 17: *The Arkansas Gazette* publishes an article by Steve Albert, who states that the previous May 12, he attended a meeting of Peace Links, which was begun by Betty Bumpers (wife of U.S. Senator Dale Bumpers) who remarked at the meeting: "At some point, perhaps we all would be in progression toward a one-world government. It's a logical progression of events. We are all one people."

1989

▪ Roger B. Porter (Rhodes Scholar 1969) becomes Assistant to the President for Economic and Domestic Policy under President Bush. He was director of the White House Office of Policy Development from 1982 to 1985 during President Reagan's administration. And after President Bush leaves office in 1993, he will be a professor of government and business at Harvard University.

▪ *Loyalties: A Son's Memoirs* by former *Washington Post* reporter Carl Bernstein is published. In this book, Carl's father (who along with Carl's mother had been members of the Communist Party in America) tells Carl: "You're going to prove [U.S. Senator Joseph] McCarthy right, because all he was saying was that the system was loaded with communists. And he was right." Further evidence that Sen. McCarthy was right will come from the Venona documents released July 11, 1995. See *The Washington Post* (March 6, 1996, p. A1) and the National Security Agency's website (*http://www.nsa.gov:8080/*).

▪ *For the Common Good* by Herman E. Daly and John B. Cobb, Jr., is published, and will be expanded in 1994. Daly has been a senior economist at the World Bank, and in this book, one reads that

> the World Court needs to be strengthened so that in the future nations such as the United States cannot ignore its judgments with impunity.... If the economy becomes more and more global, with economic decisions not controlled by any political body, then World Government in a strong sense will be needed.... The economy *must* be under some supervision. If the economy is global, global government must be instituted sooner or later.

▪ November 20: At the U.N., the United States endorses the U.N. Convention on the Rights of the Child. Early in 1993, Rhodes Scholars Sen. Bill Bradley and Sen. Richard Lugar, among others, will introduce Senate Resolution 70, which will state:

> Whereas on November 20, 1989, the United States and other members of the United Nations unanimously endorsed the United Nations Convention on the Rights of the Child and urged national governments to ratify the Convention and make possible the application of the Convention as *international law;* Whereas

> the Convention, if implemented, will help establish *universal legal standards* for the care and protection of children against neglect, exploitation, and abuse; . . . the Convention remains a force for improving the lot of children, both *in the United States* and abroad. . . . (emphasis added)

Some of the specific provisions for children's "rights" contained within the Convention, and which would be applied to American children, are ominously destructive of parental authority.

1990

▪ February 28: President Bush, in a fund-raising speech in San Francisco, states:

> Time and again in this century, the political map of the world was transformed. And in each instance, a new world order came about through the advent of a new tyrant or the outbreak of a bloody global war, or its end.

This is six months *before* Iraq's invasion of Kuwait in August.

▪ March 12: CFR member Paul Nitze delivers a speech at the opening of the new CFR office in Washington, D.C., where he says:

> For the Council on Foreign Relations to have its own quarters here in Washington reflects a changed era.

> In the '20s and '30s, New York was not only the financial, industrial and press capital of the country, but prided itself on being its policy center as well. The State Department and White House might conduct diplomacy in peace and raise and command armies in war, but policy was made by serious people, men with a longer view, i.e., the great men of finance and their advisers. New York was where they were to be found.

The CFR's headquarters had been in New York.

▪ June: The National Center on Education and the Economy (with David Rockefeller as a board member) publishes *America's Choice: high skills or low wages!*, which is a report of The Commission on the Skills of the American Workforce, chaired by Ira Magaziner (Rhodes Scholar 1969–71), who along with Hillary Rodham Clinton will lead the preparation of the Clinton administration's national health care plan. In the above-mentioned report, one reads: "a new educational performance standard should be set for all students, to be met by age 16. This standard should be established nationally and benchmarked to the highest in the world."

In an article in *Educational Leadership* (March 1992) authored by Magaziner and Hillary Rodham Clinton, they will further explain:

> Students passing a series of performance-based assessments that incorporate this new standard would be awarded a Certificate of Initial Mastery. Possession of the certificate would qualify a student to choose

> among going to work, entering a college preparatory program, or studying for a Technological and Professional Certificate.

In *The New Republic* (January 24, 1994), Jacob Weisberg (Rhodes Scholar 1987) will explain Magaziner's collectivist convictions, and state:

> Magaziner's guiding idea is that rational planning can solve any problem, social, economic, or spiritual. His universe is one in which the uncertainty principle and the law of unintended consequences do not exist; his career is testimony to the belief that for every problem there exists a total solution.

Magaziner's and Ms. Clinton's proposal is similar to what occurs in Germany, including its apprentice system, which Lester Thurow (Rhodes Scholar 1960–62) believes "is the envy of many other countries." Thurow, a leading futurist and dean of MIT's Sloan School of Management, is a forceful proponent of a new world-economic perspective calling for a great deal of change (led by the business community) in the U.S.—away from *laissez-faire* capitalism toward government-established national industrial goals with capital and labor flows directed by government to achieve them. He tells a story set in A.D. 2050 looking backward at companies becoming increasingly international, and there is a shift of power from national to regional (multinational) governments around the world.

▪ June 29: U.S. Ambassador Max Kampelman during his plenary remarks at the Copenhagen meeting of the Conference on Security and Cooperation in Europe (CSCE) states:

> This suggests . . . the need to reappraise traditional understandings of sovereignty. That process is already well underway. Nations are, by agreement, curtailing their sovereign power over many domestic and security affairs. . . . States have recognized the right of other States to evaluate their internal behavior.

▪ Summer/Fall: Writing in the World Federalist Association's newsletter, deputy director Eric Cox describes world events over the past year or two, and declares:

> It's sad but true that the slow-witted American press has not grasped the significance of most of these developments. But most federalists know what is happening. . . . And they are not frightened by the old bug-a-boo of sovereignty.

▪ September 11: President Bush delivers an address to Congress titled "Toward a New World Order," regarding the crisis in the Persian Gulf after Iraq invaded Kuwait in August. He will follow this with an October 1 address to the U.N., in which he will speak of the "collective strength of the world community expressed by the U.N. . . . a historic movement towards a new world order."

▪ October: President Bush's nominee for the U.S. Supreme Court, David Souter (Rhodes Scholar 1961–63), is confirmed by the U.S. Senate. Though supposedly a conservative, he will render quite a few non-conservative decisions.

▪ Edwin Yoder (Rhodes Scholar 1958), a member of *The Washington Post* Writer's Group, authors *The Unmaking of a Whig*, in which he takes "cheap shots" at fundamentalists.

▪ The Prince of Wales Business Leaders Forum holds its organizational meeting, called "Stakeholders: The Challenge in a Global Market," in Charleston, South Carolina. It will operate in twenty-six countries and hold international meetings involving five thousand corporate, governmental, and non-governmental leaders, fostering many different types of partnerships on a global basis. For more information on this see Joan Veon's *Prince Charles: The Sustainable Prince* (Hearthstone Publishing, Ltd.).

1991

▪ CFR member Neil Rudenstine (Rhodes Scholar 1956–59) becomes president of Harvard University and will say the school needs to become more engaged in social service, particularly in health policy and the environment. He will tell General Colin Powell "we disagree profoundly" on allowing homosexuals in the military.

▪ Jeff Shesol becomes a Rhodes Scholar and then one of the top nationally syndicated cartoonists, with his "Thatch" cartoon strip in one hundred and fifty newspapers.

▪ June 22: *The Economist* (which has been influenced by The Group) editorializes in "The World Order Changeth" that

> America itself needs to remember that a willingness to involve others is not enough to make a collective world order work. There must also be readiness to submit to it. If America really wants such an order, it will have to be ready to . . . submit itself to the International Court . . . (and) make a habit of consulting the U.N. Is it ready to do so?

▪ Late July: On a Cable News Network program, CFR member and former CIA director Stansfield Turner (Rhodes Scholar 1947–50), when asked about Iraq, responds:

> We have a much bigger objective. We've got to look at the long run here. This is an example—the situation between the United Nations and Iraq—where the United Nations is deliberately intruding into the sovereignty of a sovereign nation. . . . Now this is a marvelous precedent (to be used in) all countries of the world. . . .

▪ October 23: Bill Clinton delivers his first (one of three) "New Covenant" speech at Georgetown University, where he will praise his former mentor there, Prof. Carroll Quigley, just as he will the next year during his acceptance speech at the Democratic National Convention. During Clinton's campaign his theme will be a "New

Covenant" vision, which were the exact words of a concept presented by Jeremy Rifkin, organizer of the first national rally against the Vietnam War (also opposed by Clinton) in 1967, and Ted Howard in *The Emerging Order* (1979). In their book, Rifkin and Howard suggested that perhaps the only way for America to avoid becoming a "fascist society . . . (with) Christian doctrine made an adjunct to right-wing and capitalist policies" would be to embrace the concept of a "new covenant vision," NCV (an economically, ecologically, etc., steady-state society).

- *Beyond Interdependence: The Meshing of the World's Economy and the Earth's Ecology* by Jim MacNeill is published by Oxford University Press, with the Foreword by David Rockefeller and the Introduction by Maurice Strong.

1992

- Jonah Martin Edelman is selected as a Rhodes Scholar. He is the son of Marian Wright Edelman, the leftist president of the Children's Defense Fund, of which Hillary Clinton has been chairman.

- May 4: *Newsweek* publishes "Clinton's Rhodes Brain Trust" by Clara Bingham. Writing about Clinton's Rhodes Scholar "Oxford brotherhood" (e.g., Strobe Talbott, Robert Reich, Ira Magaziner, *et al*), she states:

> They began what Clinton and his clique somewhat pretentiously call "the Conversation." The topics vary, but the Conversation boils down to a discussion of how to save the world.

▪ June 3–14: The United Nations Conference on Environment and Development (UNCED), or Earth Summit, is held in Rio de Janeiro, Brazil. *Agenda 21* is the Programme of Action adopted by consensus by 178 governments at the UNCED, and it is envisioned as the "blueprint for action for global sustainable development into the 21st century." It covers a wide range of economic and environmental issues.

▪ June 14: On ABC's "This Week with David Brinkley," former top Reagan advisor Michael Deaver announced that "in five years, we're going to have a World Parliament."

▪ July 20: *Time* magazine publishes "The Birth of the Global Nation" by Strobe Talbott (Rhodes Scholar roommate of Bill Clinton at Oxford University, CFR director, Carnegie Endowment for International Peace board of directors member, and Trilateralist from a wealthy Ohio banking family), in which he writes:

> All countries are basically social arrangements. . . . No matter how permanent or even sacred they may seem at any one time, in fact they are all artificial and temporary. . . . Perhaps national sovereignty wasn't such a great idea after all. . . . But it has taken the events in our own wondrous and terrible century to clinch the case for world government.

Talbott as an editor of *Time* will defend Clinton during this presidential campaign year, and eventually he will be appointed by President Clinton as the number two person at the State Department (behind Secretary of State Warren Christopher, former Trilateralist and former CFR vice-chairman and director), and he will be confirmed by about two-thirds of the U.S. Senate despite his statement regarding the unimportance of national sovereignty. During the 1992 presidential campaign, Clinton will also be defended by Michael Kinsley (Rhodes Scholar 1972–74) of *The New Republic*, who also serves as moderator of "Firing Line" hosted by William F. Buckley, Jr. (CFR member, and member of "Skull and Bones," who believes certain drugs like marijuana should be decriminalized).

▪ August 26: *The New York Times* (influenced by the American branch of The Group) publishes "The World Needs an Army on Call" by U.S. Senator David Boren (Rhodes Scholar 1963, CFR member, and member of "Skull and Bones"), in which he states:

> In the aftermath of World War II, President Truman wanted to empower the United Nations to create a new world order. . . . Richard Gardner proposes that forty to fifty member nations contribute to a rapid-deployment force of one hundred thousand volunteers that could train under common leadership.[26] . . . It is time for us to create such a force. . . . The existence of such a force would go a long way toward making the "new world order" more than just a slogan.

▪ *The Twilight of Sovereignty* by CFR member (and former Citicorp chairman) Walter Wriston is published, in which he claims: "A truly global economy will require . . . compromise of national sovereignty. . . . There is no escaping the system."

▪ September 27 and 29: CBS's "60 Minutes" on September 27 and ABC's "Nightline" on September 29 show how the U.S. Agency for International Development has been using tax dollars to promote the movement of U.S. businesses to Central America, resulting in a loss of certain jobs. This would facilitate a new world economic order. When President Bush was asked in the Carolinas about the loss of textile jobs, he said *"C'est la vie"* ("That's life").

▪ September 29: At a town hall meeting in Los Angeles, Trilateralist and former CFR president (and "Skull and Bones" member) Winston Lord delivers a speech titled, "Changing Our Ways: America and the New World," in which he remarks: "To a certain extent, we are going to have to yield some of our sovereignty, which will be controversial at home. . . . (Under) the North American Free Trade Agreement (NAFTA) . . . some Americans are going to be hurt as low-wage jobs are taken away." Lord will become an Assistant Secretary of State in the Clinton administration.

▪ November: President Bush (former CFR member and Trilateralist, and member of "Skull and Bones") loses the presidential election to Governor Bill Clinton (Rhodes Scholar, CFR member, and Trilateralist). Both candidates supported such things as the New World Order and NAFTA, but there are reasons the elitist network of power wanted Clinton to replace Bush. Domestically, further Bush appointments to the Supreme Court might jeopardize rulings such as *Roe v. Wade* concerning abortion rights.

President Clinton's appointees to the U.S. Supreme Court will be Stephen Breyer (a Marshall Scholar in Britain) and Ruth Ginsburg, who are two of only three CFR members on the U.S. Court of Appeals (about one hundred and fifty total members), which is probably not a coincidence.

Internationally, only with a Democrat in the White House could enough Democrats in the U.S. House of Representatives be persuaded to vote for NAFTA (just forty percent voted for it), so that it could pass. This will be an essential part of the globalists' plan to link eventually (perhaps under GATT, General Agreement on Tariffs and Trade, or the World Trade Organization)[27] an expanded NAFTA (including all of Latin America) with the already existing EC (European Community) and the expected Asia-Pacific trade agreement, all of which will have to be managed, they believe, by a world government under their control. Bill Clinton is the first Rhodes Scholar elected President of the United States, but Rhodes Scholars have preceded him as prime ministers of Canada, Australia, Jamaica, and Malta.

Just as both President Bush (Republican) and President Clinton (Democrat) supported NAFTA, they also support GATT, which will pass Congress even though a majority of the American public oppose them. Relevant in this regard is Prof. Quigley's comment in *Tragedy and Hope* that

> the chief problem of American political life for a long time has been how to make the two Congressional parties more national and international. The argument that the two parties should represent opposed ideals and policies, one, perhaps, of the Right and the other of the Left, is a foolish idea. . . . Instead, the two parties should be almost identical, so that the American people can "throw the rascal out" at any election without leading to any profound or extensive shifts in policy.

This reminds one of author Lewis Carroll's characters "Tweedledee" and "Tweedledum." Also possibly instructive here, regarding the role of transnational corporations in the passage of NAFTA and GATT, is what Prof. Quigley wrote about the political influence of business interests in the late nineteenth century. He said:

> They expected that they would be able to control both political parties equally. Indeed, some of them intended to contribute to both and to allow an alternation of the two parties in public office in order to conceal their own influence, inhibit any exhibition of independence by politicians, and allow the electorate to believe that they were exercising their own free choice.

▪ November 11: National Center on Education and the Economy (NCEE) president Marc Tucker writes a letter to NCEE board member Hillary Clinton saying he has recently been in the office of NCEE board member David

Rockefeller, who was celebrating Bill Clinton's election as president of the U.S. Tucker explains how this will give them a chance to implement their plan to integrate education into a human resources development system

> that literally extends from cradle to grave and is the same system for everyone—young and old, poor and rich. . . . Radical changes in attitudes, values and beliefs are required to move any combination of these agendas. . . .

This same year, Tucker co-authors *Thinking for a Living* with NCEE board member Ray Marshall, Secretary of Labor under President Jimmy Carter. In this book, they state that many of the former members of the communist bloc in Eastern Europe and the Soviet Union "have done a better job than we of building effective human-resource development programs."

▪ December 7: *The Christian Science Monitor* (which has been influenced by The Group) publishes "A Rhodes Scholar Reaches the Top" by Robert Rotberg (Rhodes Scholar 1957, and author of *The Founder: Cecil Rhodes and the Pursuit of Power*). In this article, Rotberg writes:

> Rhodes was a man of unparalleled vision. . . . Mr. Clinton's accession to the American presidency fulfills Rhodes' deepest aspiration. . . . Rhodes believed that he had discovered an idea that could lead "to the cessation of all wars and one language throughout the world." Rhodes also specified fairly clearly the kinds

> of men who should receive the opportunity to go to Oxford. He had Clinton in mind. . . . They were to "esteem the performance of public duties" as their highest aim. Rhodes wanted the best men for "the World's fight.". . . In the ninety years of scholarships, only Clinton has taken Rhodes' dreams to the top.

- December 14: *The Nation* publishes an article by Christopher Hitchens, who was a contemporary of 1968 Rhodes Scholars Bill Clinton, Strobe Talbott, and Robert Reich (the latter of whom claims that he introduced Hillary Rodham to Bill Clinton). Though not a Rhodes Scholar himself, Hitchens attended Balliol College at Oxford University, where George Stephanopoulos was a Rhodes Scholar in 1984. In this article, the author describes how Clinton has surrounded himself with other Rhodes Scholars, and he comments:

> A Rhodesian formation imparts a definite sense of knowing what is best . . . for others. It has helped bestow a patina of refinement on the raw exercise of power, and has shaped the contours of the permanent party of government as it exists in law, lobbying, business, intelligence, diplomacy and the military. . . . In (George Bush's) establishment heart, he must have realized that nothing is more calculated than a Rhodes background to assure a smooth and equable transition.

On C-Span television (August 23, 1993), the self-described socialist Hitchens will state: "It is, of course, the case that there is a ruling class in this country, and that it has allies internationally."

▪ *Kissinger: A Biography* by Walter Isaacson (Rhodes Scholar 1974–76) is published. Isaacson is an editor for *Time,* and on December 10, 1993, he will write a letter to authors Thomas and Kathleen Schaeper, stating: "Both as a journalist and biographer, I've been surprised how often all the glories of Locke-Berkeley-Hume-Kant turned out to be not only interesting but useful." Former Secretary of State Henry Kissinger (CFR member, Trilateralist, and Bilderberger) as a student was very interested in Immanuel Kant, who in 1795 authored *Perpetual Peace* proposing a federated "world republic" with a "world citizenship."

▪ December 31: *The New York Times* publishes "The New Year at a New Age Retreat: The Clintons in Agreeable Company" by Michael Kelly.

1992–93

▪ Winter: The CFR's *Foreign Affairs* publishes "Empowering the United Nations" by U.N. Secretary-General Boutros Boutros-Ghali, who asserts:

> It is undeniable that the centuries-old doctrine of absolute and exclusive sovereignty no longer stands. . . . Underlying the rights of the individual and the rights of peoples is a dimension of universal sovereignty that resides in all humanity. . . . It is a sense that increasingly finds expression in the gradual expansion of in-

> ternational law. . . . In this setting the significance of the United Nations should be evident and accepted.

1993

▪ January 13: Confirmation hearings are held for CFR member Warren Christopher's nomination to be Secretary of State. He and Senator Joseph Biden discuss the possibility of NATO becoming a peacekeeping surrogate for the U.N. "to foster the creation of a new world order."

▪ January 25: *Newsweek* publishes "The New Age President" by Howard Fineman, in which he writes:

> America gets a New Age president this week. . . . He can search for the inner self while seeking connectedness with the greater whole. . . . Clinton talks from time to time in the lingo of "centering" the personality and "channeling" creative personal energy. . . . For Clinton, "talking it through" is . . . a method of leadership, as though government were nothing more or less than a giant national counseling session . . . a group-therapy exercise. . . .

▪ Some of the Rhodes Scholars appointed by President Clinton are: Robert Reich (Secretary of Labor), Michael Warren (special assistant to the Chief-of-Staff and Secretary of Labor), Thomas Williamson (Department of Labor chief counsel), James Woolsey (CIA Director), George Stephanopoulos (Communications Director, who had formerly worked for U.S. Rep. Edward Feighan, then worked for Michael Dukakis' presidential campaign as Communications Director, and then worked for House Majority Leader Richard Gephardt as executive assistant), Ira Magaziner (Senior Advisor for Policy Development and for whom future Israeli Prime Minister Benjamin Netanyahu had earlier worked), Strobe Talbott (Ambassador-at-large and Special Advisor to the Secretary of State on the New Independent States and Russia), Stephen Oxman (Assistant Secretary of State for European Affairs), Walter Slocombe (Deputy Undersecretary of Defense for Policy), Sarah Sewall (Deputy Assistant Secretary of Defense for Peacekeeping/Peacemaking Policy), Ashton Carter (Assistant Secretary of Defense for Program Analysis and Evaluation), Susan Rice (National Security Council), Joseph Nye (head of the National Intelligence Council), Richard Gardner (Ambassador to Spain), Jack Davison (Ambassador to Niger), Bonnie St. John Deane (Director of the National Economic Council), W. Bowman Cutter (National Economic Council deputy assistant), Sylvia Matthews (an aide to the National Economic Council who will be White House Deputy Chief-of-Staff), Bruce Reed (Domestic Policy Council deputy assistant, who had been Clinton's campaign-issues director and former policy director for the Democratic Leadership Council), Kevin Thurm (HHS chief-of-staff), Daniel Porterfield (an HHS speechwriter), Atul Gawande (HHS), and Renee Stone (EPA).

Of the aforementioned, Thomas Williamson, James Woolsey, George Stephanopoulos, Strobe Talbott, Stephen Oxman, Walter Slocombe, Sarah Sewall, Ashton Carter, Joseph Nye, Richard Gardner, and W. Bowman

Cutter are CFR members, with Nye (Rhodes Scholar 1958–60) and Gardner also being Trilateralists. Two other Clinton appointees, Mike Espy (Secretary of Agriculture) and Joycelyn Elders (Surgeon-General), have served on Rhodes Scholarship selection committees, with the expressed views of Elders on several moral issues being especially objectionable.

Ira Magaziner will help Hillary Clinton develop a health care reform plan in 1993 that noted economist Milton Friedman will characterize as socialistic, and in December 1997 U.S. District Court Judge Royce Lamberth will rule that Magaziner misled a court about the participation of the private sector or special interest groups in the development of the health care reform plan. Lamberth will order a $286,000 court sanction. While at Oxford, Magaziner had attended seminars at the London School of Economics (founded by the Fabian Socialists) and had helped to organize some anti-Vietnam War rallies in London.

▪ March 21: *The New York Times* publishes the article, "Rhodes to Rhodes: On the Inside Looking In," by Douglas Jehl (Rhodes Scholar 1984), in which he writes:

> "They seem to be everywhere," said Senator John H. Chafee, the Rhode Island Republican, who at a recent confirmation hearing found himself staring down at a witness table lined with nothing but Rhodes Scholars.

▪ April 6: Hillary Rodham Clinton says, "Let us be willing to remold society by redefining what it means to be a human being" (see *U.S. News and World Report*, December 13, 1993). This sounds similar to the Fabian Socialists' motto: "Remould it (the world) nearer to the heart's desire." Ms. Clinton's attitude regarding "what it means to be a human being" seems clear from her advocacy of abortion rights. And the elitist insensitivity of President Clinton seems clear from his comment two weeks later (April 20), after the fire at Waco burned many men, women, and children, when the president said Attorney-General Janet Reno should not resign just "because some religious fanatics murdered themselves." During the 1992 presidential campaign, when some people angered Bill Clinton, he was quoted as saying: "I want to put a fist halfway down their throats with this. I don't want subtlety. I want their teeth on the sidewalks." These comments will be characterized as "brutal," one of Cecil Rhodes' requirements for his scholars.

▪ April 21: General Colin Powell receives the United Nations Association–USA's Global Leadership Award, and he remarks: "The United Nations will spearhead our efforts to manage the new conflicts [that afflict our world]. . . . Yes, the principles of the United Nations Charter *are* worth our lives, our fortunes, and our sacred honor."

▪ May 4: New CFR president Leslie Gelb (formerly an editor at *The New York Times)* says on "The Charlie Rose Show" that

> . . . you [Charlie Rose] had me on [before] to talk about the new world order. . . . I talk about it all the time. . . . It's one world now. . . . The Council [CFR] can find,

> nurture and begin to put people in the kinds of jobs this country needs. And that's going to be one of the major enterprises of the Council under me.

▪ June 22: In case there is any doubt about whether President Clinton supports world government, on this date he signs a letter to the World Federalist Association congratulating Strobe Talbott on receiving (June 24) the WFA's first "Norman Cousins Global Governance Award." The WFA, a leading force for world federal government, has identified Talbott as a second generation world federalist; and the late Norman Cousins (a past WFA president) once said: "World government is coming, in fact, it is inevitable. No arguments for or against it can change that fact." Former U.S. presidential candidate and current WFA president John Anderson will note on June 24 that "the same kind of progress that was destined to make us one world economically had to bring us together politically." This could represent the long held globalists' concept that regional economic alliances (like NAFTA and the European Economic Community) could be interconnected into a global economy, which would have to be managed by a world government. Anderson will say that Talbott is receiving this award for his July 20, 1992, *Time* article, "The Birth of the Global Nation," and in appreciation for what he has done "for the cause of global governance." Anderson will read President Clinton's letter, which states:

> Norman Cousins worked for world peace and world government.... Strobe Talbott's lifetime achievements

> as a voice for global harmony have earned him this recognition. . . . He will be a worthy recipient of the Norman Cousins Global Governance Award. Best wishes . . . for future success.

Not only does President Clinton use the specific term, "world government," but he also expressly wishes the WFA "future success" in pursuit of it. Talbott will proudly accept the award, but he will say the WFA should have given it to the other nominee, Mikhail Gorbachev.

In 1994 the WFA will publish *The Genius of Federation: Why World Federation Is the Answer to Global Problems,* which will state:

> Let the U.N. establish new agencies such as an International Criminal Court. . . . National sovereignty would be gradually eroded until it is no longer an issue. Eventually a world federation can be formally adopted with little resistance.

▪ July 18: CFR member and Trilateralist Henry Kissinger writes in *The Los Angeles Times* concerning NAFTA: "What Congress will have before it is not a conventional trade agreement but the architecture of a new international system . . . a first step toward a new world order."

▪ July 28: Oxford University's Rhodes House Warden Sir Anthony Kenny remarks: "Cecil Rhodes' scheme seems to be working pretty well." Is it a mere coincidence that Kenny refers to Rhodes' "scheme," and in Rhodes' 1890 letter to W. T. Stead, there is the statement: "Fancy the charm to young America . . . to share in a *scheme* to take the government of the whole world!" (emphasis added)?

- Summer: An agreement is reached between the U.N. and NATO concerning Bosnia that allows members of NATO (including the U.S.) "no right to reject a United Nations request for air strikes when its troops are in danger." On April 3, 1994, Secretary of Defense William Perry will seem to rule out military action to save the town of Gorazde, a "safe area" where U.N. troops are located, and he will be supported on April 5 by the chairman of the Joint Chiefs of Staff. However, on April 9, U.N. Secretary-General Boutros Boutros-Ghali will warn the Serbian forces to pull back from Gorazde or face air strikes. On April 10 and 11 American F-16s will strike Serbian forces, and *The New York Times* will state that President Clinton "reviewed the American policy at length on Thursday and Friday (April 7 and 8), but noted that the rules that NATO approved took any decision to launch an attack out of his hands." On April 11, chief operations officer for the Joint Chiefs of Staff, Lt. General Jack Sheehan, will emphasize that the United Nations is setting the rules. And on April 23, the U.N. will veto NATO's request to launch air strikes against the Serbs.

- September 9: Concerning whether U.S. troops should remain in Somalia as part of a U.N. operation, General Colin Powell, chairman of the Joint Chiefs of Staff, says that a pullout would be "devastating to our hopes for the new world order and our ability to participate in multinational organizations to deal with problems like this."

▪ October 19: President Clinton says that his administration is engaging in a political process regarding Somalia "to see how we can . . . do all the things the United Nations ordered us to do."

▪ October 30: *The Washington Post* ombudsman Richard Harwood describes on its op-ed page the role of the CFR's press and media members in the following manner: "Their membership is an acknowledgment of their ascension into the American ruling class (where) they do not merely analyze and interpret foreign policy for the United States; they help make it."

▪ W. Scott Thompson (Rhodes Scholar 1963–66) writes "Conflict and Conflict Resolution: On to the Twenty-First Century" for the federal United States Institute of Peace, of which he is a board member appointed by President Reagan in 1986. In this article, Thompson writes about

> a positive factor: the greater reliance on (and opportunity for) the United Nations to resolve perennial conflicts. . . . In addition to a strengthened U.N., a New World Order requires understandings and divisions of labor among like-minded friends across the globe.

Thompson also was an Assistant Secretary of Defense, 1975–76.

▪ *Fire with Fire: The New Female Power and How It Will Change the 21st Century* by Naomi Wolf (Rhodes Scholar 1984–87) is published, in which she promotes "power feminism." Wolf will encourage women to "become goddesses of disobedience."

1994

▪ January/February: The CFR's *Foreign Affairs* prints an opening article by CFR senior fellow Michael Clough, in which he writes that the "Wise Men" (e.g., Paul Nitze, Dean Acheson, George Kennan, and John J. McCloy) have

> assiduously guarded it [American foreign policy] for the past fifty years. . . . They ascended to power during World War II. . . . This was as it should be. National security and the national interest, they argued, must transcend the special interests and passions of the people who make up America. . . . How was this small band of Atlantic-minded internationalists able to triumph? . . . Eastern internationalists were able to shape and staff the burgeoning foreign policy institutions. . . . As long as the Cold War endured and nuclear Armageddon seemed only a missile away, the public was willing to tolerate such an undemocratic foreign policy making system.

As an example of how the elitists have been involved with both sides (e.g. Nazi and communist), McCloy sat in Hitler's box at the 1936 Olympics and in late July 1961 was swimming and smiling with Nikita Khrushchev at the Black Sea.[28]

▪ March 27: *The New York Times* publishes an article by Theodore Forstmann, who writes:

> For the first time, more Americans are employed by Government—18.7 million—than by manufacturing—18.1 million. . . . The United States, unfortunately, is moving toward democratic socialism. . . . And the Clinton administration—which sees no task as too small, no dream too large, no issue too delicate for probing Government hands—has clearly joined the statist camp.

▪ March/April: The CFR's *Foreign Affairs* publishes Paul Krugman's "Competitiveness: A Dangerous Obsession," about which the journal's editor notes:

> In our lead essay, noted economist Paul Krugman asserts that this "competitiveness hypothesis" is not only utterly unsupported by data but that thinking in such terms leads to bad public policy on a range of issues from trade to health care.

If the globalists are pursuing a World Socialist Government via a one-world economic (including trade) system, then cooperation is desired over the instability of competition (the *Foreign Affairs* editor's note above is titled, "Order from Chaos"). The CFR often reveals through its publications what is planned for the future, and in this case, it's cooperativeness replacing competitiveness. Concerning "health care" mentioned previously, this is why the current discussion of a future health care plan emphasizes the "cooperativeness" typical of socialist plans over the "competitiveness" (to hold down costs, etc.) of the current capitalist system. To prepare the next generation for the planned future, not only are non–competitive sports being promoted among youth, but so is outcome-based education's "cooperative learning" in groups with group grades (socialism emphasizes "the group").

▪ April 14: Americans are killed as a result of a "friendly fire" attack while patrolling over Iraq, and Vice-President Al Gore will refer to them as "those who died in the service of the United Nations."

▪ May 3: President Clinton signs Presidential Decision Directive 25, which strengthens the U.N. and describes how American soldiers will serve under foreign commanders. PDD 25 will only be released to top administration officials and a few members of Congress.

▪ July 24–26: Harlan Cleveland (Rhodes Scholar 1938 and CFR member) is on the board of directors of the World Future Society (WFS), which is holding its annual conference titled "Toward the New Millennium: Living, Learning, and Working" during which Cleveland is participating in a facilitated discussion by the "World 2000 Project" team (group), of which he is a member. Also on the board of directors of the WFS is Trilateralist and CFR member Robert S. McNamara. The WFS has held seven general assemblies—meetings of futurists from around the world—and a number of specialized conferences (since its founding in 1966), including "Business and the Future" and "Creating the 21st Century: Institutions and Social Change."

■ August 25: On CBS' "This Morning" is described a new supercomputer soon coming to the U.S. It is named "GOD," and contains all vital medical statistics, so that it can determine whether patients should be kept alive or not, based upon health and economic factors.

■ August 28: On ABC's "This Week with David Brinkley," commentator Cokie Roberts casually remarks: "Global bankers are really running the world."

■ August 29: C. Dean Rhody, director of resource management for the Department of the Army's headquarters for training and doctrine command at Fort Monroe, Virginia, issues a memorandum regarding "Draft Army

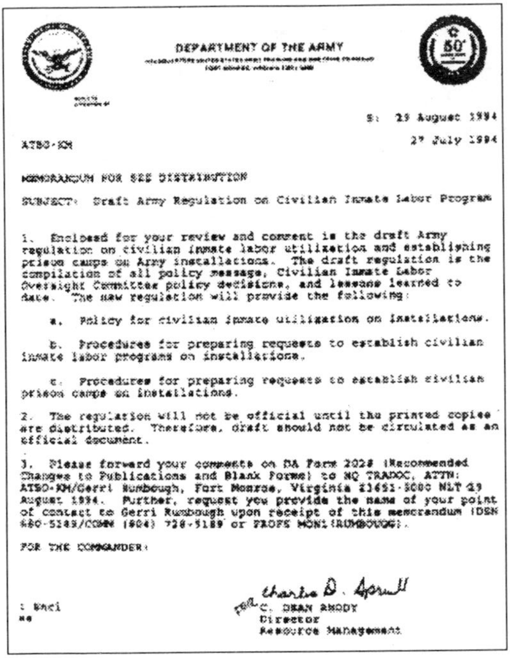

DEPARTMENT OF THE ARMY

S: 29 August 1994

ATSO-KM

27 July 1994

MEMORANDUM FOR SEE DISTRIBUTION

SUBJECT: Draft Army Regulation on Civilian Inmate Labor Program

1. Enclosed for your review and comment is the draft Army regulation on civilian inmate labor utilization and establishing prison camps on Army installations. The draft regulation is the compilation of all policy message, Civilian Inmate Labor Oversight Committee policy decisions, and lessons learned to date. The new regulation will provide the following:

a. Policy for civilian inmate utilization on installations.

b. Procedures for preparing requests to establish civilian inmate labor programs on installations.

c. Procedures for preparing requests to establish civilian prison camps on installations.

2. The regulation will not be official until the printed copies are distributed. Therefore, draft should not be circulated as an official document.

3. Please forward your comments on DA Form 2028 (Recommended Changes to Publications and Blank Forms) to HQ TRADOC, ATTN: ATSO-KM/Gerri Rumbough, Fort Monroe, Virginia 23651-5000 NLT 29 August 1994. Further, request you provide the name of your point of contact to Gerri Rumbough upon receipt of this memorandum (DSN 680-5149/COMM (804) 728-5189 or PROFS MON1(RUMBOUGG).

FOR THE COMMANDER:

1 Encl
as

FOR C. DEAN RHODY
Director
Resource Management

Regulation on Civilian Inmate Labor Program," including "procedures for preparing requests to establish civilian prison camps on installations." Supposedly, these prison camps on military installations would just be to house civilian inmates from states' overcrowded prisons. However, it is worth remembering in this regard that during the Oliver North hearing in Congress, Rep. Jack Brooks stated: "I read in several papers that there had been developed a contingency plan, in the event of an emergency by the National Security Council that would suspend the American Constitution." Commenting on this later, Rep. Henry Gonzalez will say:

> The truth of the matter is that you do have those standby provisions, and the statutory emergency plans are there whereby you could, in the name of stopping terrorism, apprehend, invoke the military, and arrest Americans and hold them in detention camps.

- November 8: According to the *Daily Universe,* Brigham Young University's campus newspaper, former U.S. government official Lawrence Eagleburger, speaking at a BYU forum on this date, declares that the U.S.

> can either become the world policeman, or an international policing force must be established with adequate authority and force to maintain world peace. . . . We have to be the world's thought policemen to create a world police force.

Eagleburger is a CFR member and a member of Kissinger Associates.

▪ November 15: Felix Rohatyn testifies before the Senate Commerce Committee regarding GATT, and indicates that powerful international interests have already planned on GATT's passage and have invested accordingly. He warns that if GATT does not pass, there will be dire economic consequences. Rohatyn is a CFR member, Trilateralist, and co-partner with Lazard Brothers investment bankers. The managing director of Lazard Brothers since 1963 (Adam Marris) and before 1963 (Lord Robert Brand) were also head of Round Table Groups set up by Lord Alfred Milner as part of Cecil Rhodes' plan for world dominion. Rohatyn will be U.S. Ambassador to France.

▪ November 20: Milton Friedman, speaking on C-Span on the fiftieth anniversary reissue of F. A. Hayek's 1944 book *The Road to Serfdom*, says:

> Socialism guides our behavior. . . . In practice, we keep moving down the Socialist road. . . . In fact, we are more than half Socialist today, that is, more than half the total output of the country is being distributed in a way that is determined by the government (including regulations). . . . Bill Clinton is a Socialist, defined as somebody who believes that the way to achieve good things is to have government do it. You can't think of a more Socialist program than the health care program that he tried to get us to adopt.

The Clinton administration health care program was actually developed by Hillary Clinton and Ira Magaziner (Rhodes Scholar).

▪ December 29: *The New York Times* indicates CIA Director James Woolsey (Rhodes Scholar 1963) is leaving the Clinton administration, and *The New York Times* (October 28, 1996) will indicate that Woolsey "has endorsed Bob Dole" for president.

1995

▪ January: Early this month, *The New York Times* Special Features sends over its wires an article by CFR president Leslie Gelb (a shortened version of his article in the CFR's *Foreign Affairs,* November-December 1994), in which he writes:

> The very long process of shaping a more effective and responsible United Nations must begin. This will require some sacrifices of sovereignty. . . . Multilateralism . . . is a fact not to be debated, but absorbed into American strategy.

▪ January 27: Billionaire financier George Soros at the World Economic Forum at Davos, Switzerland, says the world needs a "new world order," and he further warns: "I am here to alert you that we are entering a period of world disorder." Soros received his B.S. degree in 1952 from the London School of Economics (U.S. Treasury Secretary Robert Rubin, former head of Goldman Sachs international bankers, also did graduate work there in

1960–61), which was established by Fabian Socialists. Soros also heads a CFR task force on U.N. reform, and in the near future will attack several Asian currencies, resulting in the International Monetary Fund (IMF) bailing them out, but with financial strings attached (e.g., in Thailand the IMF has demanded an increase in domestic taxes, among other things, in exchange for its loans to that nation). Soros also reportedly has spent and will spend millions of dollars on groups advocating marijuana legalization.

▪ February 7: Although Rush Limbaugh on several occasions has ridiculed conspiracy theories, on his national program this date, he states:

> You see, if you amount to anything in Washington these days, it is because you have been plucked or handpicked from an Ivy League school—Harvard, Yale, Kennedy School of Government—you've shown an aptitude to be a good Ivy League type, and so you're plucked so-to-speak, and you are assigned success. You are assigned a certain role in government somewhere, and then your success is monitored and tracked, and you go where the pluckers and the handpickers can put you.

Also on Limbaugh's February 7 radio program, he admits that he had denied to syndicated columnist Robert Novak that he had a phone conversation with Trilateralist Federal Reserve chairman Alan Greenspan regarding the Mexico bailout plan, even though the phone conversation did take place. Greenspan had called Limbaugh at the urging of U.S. House Speaker Newt Gingrich just before Greenspan's testimony to Congress regarding the bailout plan. On his March 8 program, Limbaugh will call the Clinton administration "Socialist Utopians."

▪ May 4: *The Seattle Times* publishes an article by nationally syndicated columnist Alexander Cockburn, who also writes for the left-wing magazine, *The Nation*. In this article, Cockburn expresses his belief that

> there is, in emerging outline, a world government composed of the International Monetary Fund and the central banks of the leading industrial nations. National sovereignty is being eroded, most recently by the GATT treaty. Liberties are under threat, as now displayed by Clinton's anti-terrorism package. Politics in America are so decayed, so rotted out, that the surprise is not that there are patriot militias but that there aren't more of them.

▪ May 31–June 6: In an article, "One World, Under Gorby" in *The San Francisco Weekly*, Gorbachev Foundation/USA president Jim Garrison states: "Over the next twenty to thirty years, we are going to end up with world government. It's inevitable." The Gorbachev Foundation USA (now called State of the World Forum) is located at the Presidio, the former prestigious American military base in San Francisco.

▪ *The Confidence Game: How Unelected Central Bankers Are Governing the Changed Global Economy* is published. It is written by Steven Solomon, a former staff reporter for *Forbes* magazine.

▪ July 20: In Milwaukee Secretary of Labor Robert Reich (Rhodes Scholar 1968) remarks: "What is an American company? I don't even know what an American company is. You have companies in your states that are now—most of them—global networks of companies." This is similar to his statements in his *The Work of Nations* (1991), where he explained:

> As borders become ever more meaningless in economic terms . . . there will be no *national* products or technologies, no national corporations, no national industries. . . . Each nation's primary political task will be to cope with the centrifugal forces of the global economy which tear at the ties binding citizens together.

▪ *Managing Globalization in the Age of Interdependence* by George C. Lodge is published. He is a CFR member, a trustee of the Carnegie Endowment for International Peace, and the son of Henry Cabot Lodge, Jr. He claims in this book that "the old systems of governance, centered on the nation–state, are inadequate. . . . An erosion of national sovereignty . . . seems inevitable," and he advocates transnational governmental mechanisms. The Editor's Preface to the book is written by leading educator Warren Bennis who, in *The Temporary Society,* stated:

> One cannot permit submission to parental authority if one wishes to bring about profound social change.

> . . . One must teach them [children] not to respect their tradition-bound elders, who are tied to the past and know only what is irrelevant.

▪ July-August: In the CFR's *Foreign Affairs*, prominent CFR member Arthur Schlesinger, Jr. exclaims: "We are not going to achieve a new world order without paying for it in blood as well as in words and money."

▪ August 22: Congressman Mel Reynolds (Rhodes Scholar 1975) is found guilty of obstruction of justice and on twelve counts of having sex with a sixteen-year-old girl in 1992.

▪ September 24: *The Washington Post* publishes an article, "Global Chic: Gorby's Bash by the Bay," in which writer George Cothran states that

> maybe challenging the powers-that-be isn't Gorbachev's main objective. Rather than disrupting the hide-bound elites that run the world, the former Soviet president seems more intent on rejoining their exclusive club.

At Gorbachev's State of the World Forum (September 27–October 1), speaker Sam Keen evokes loud applause when he states, "If we cut the world's population by ninety percent, there won't be enough people left to do ecological damage." Think about what it would take to reduce the world's population by ninety percent!

At this same State of the World Forum, Zbigniew Brzezinski declares:

> We cannot leap into world government through one quick step. A consensual global system requires a process. . . . The precondition for eventual and genuine globalization is progressive regionalization because by that we move toward larger, more stable, more cooperative units.

▪ The report, "Our Global Neighborhood," by The Commission on Global Governance (partly funded by the U.N. Development Program and endorsed by the U.N. Secretary-General) is released, and states:

> A new world order must be organized. . . . Global governance is the way we manage global affairs. . . . Nations have to accept that in certain fields, sovereignty has to be exercised collectively. . . . We need to accept that there may be circumstances within countries when the security of people is so severely violated that external intervention becomes justified. We propose that the U.N. Charter be amended to permit intervention in such circumstances. . . . We believe that there is a need for a highly trained U.N. Volunteer (military) Force. . . . Accelerated progress must be made toward demilitarizing the international society. . . . We strongly endorse community initiatives to . . . encourage the disarming of civilians. . . . The inadequacy and unreliability of present arrangements for financing the U.N. have led to proposals for a system to raise part of the resources for global governance through international taxes. . . . Acceptance of the compulsory jurisdiction of the World Court should surely be a basic

> condition for membership in the United Nations. . . . One way is to make international law enforceable in domestic courts. . . . We are . . . in need of a mobilizing principle. . . . That principle could well be global governance, a genuine internationalism, a new world order that secures the ascendancy of global neighborhood values over divisive nationalism.

▪ December 21: The United States and the European Community sign an agreement calling for "improving the quality of human resource development. . . . Transatlantic student mobility, . . . and thus portability of academic credits." As part of this New Transatlantic Agenda (NTA), the U.S. and European Union will convene a major conference, "Bridging the Atlantic: People-to-People Links," on May 5–6, 1997, calling for "thematic networks for curriculum development," and further stating that in an information-based global economy "governments are too obliged to adapt the economic, training, and social welfare programs." And on May 18, 1998, the White House will release a statement at the conclusion of the U.S.–European Summit in London, indicating that "through the New Transatlantic Agenda, created in 1995, the United States and the European Union have focused on addressing the challenges and opportunities of global integration." This will be relevant to international school-to-work initiatives.

1996

▪ January 24: U.S. Army Specialist Michael New is convicted at a court-martial on a charge of refusing an order to wear U.N. insignia.

▪ April 12: Franklin Raines (Rhodes Scholar 1971) becomes director of the federal Office of Management and Budget. He is a CFR member who has been vice-chairman of "Fannie Mae" (Federal National Mortgage Association) from 1991 to 1996, and he has also been senior vice-president of Lazard Brothers & Co., international bankers, New York City.

▪ May 6: Former CIA Director William Colby is found mysteriously dead. A few years earlier, he told a friend:

> Sometimes, there are forces too powerful for us to whip them individually, in the time frame that we would like. . . . The best we might be able to do sometimes, is to point out the truth and then step aside. That is where I think you are now. For your own personal safety and survival, step aside.

Although Colby was advising his friend about a domestic exposé of immorality, it seems clear that Colby's use of the word "we" means he has personal knowledge of these "forces too powerful." This is important in that one might consider what could cause the former director of the CIA of the most powerful nation on earth to say there are "forces too powerful."

▪ May 11: Journalist Joan Veon interviews David C. Korten, author of *When Corporations Rule the World* (1995) and former Ford Foundation project specialist in Manila. In this interview, Korten claims that

> the World Trade Organization is creating a world government in which one organization which is totally unelected, wholly secretive . . . with the power to virtually override any local or national laws if those in any way inconvenience global corporations. . . . It was a terrible shock (to those of us who supported Bill Clinton) when Clinton came in and GATT and NAFTA became the centerpieces of his policy. . . . And in a sense, there was almost a seamless transition from President Bush to President Clinton in that regard. . . . Our democracy has been rendered meaningless by big money. The truth is there are politicians [who] are owned lock, stock and barrel by the big money interests. . . . Our elections create, to some extent, a facade of choice.

▪ *The Clash of Civilizations and the Remaking of World Order* by Samuel Huntington (CFR member) is published, and on the back of the book jacket is an endorsement by Richard Bernstein in *The New York Times*, which reads: "A benchmark for informed speculation on those always fascinating questions: . . . What hidden hand is controlling our destiny? . . ." In this book, Huntington says that states (nations)

> are suffering losses in sovereignty, functions, and power. International institutions now assert the right to judge and to constrain what states do in their territory. . . . All these developments have led many to see the gradual end of the hard, "billiard ball" state . . . and the emergence of a varied, complex, multilayer

> international order more closely resembling that of medieval times.

▪ *Bold New World: The Essential Road Map to the Twenty-First Century* by William Knoke is published, in which he projects that

> our passion for the large nation state, for which our ancestors fought with their blood, will dwindle to the same emotional consequences of county or province today. A new spirit of global citizenship will evolve in its place, and with it the ascendancy of global governance.

This, along with the comment quoted above from Huntington's book, gives support to the view that there will be a techno-feudal future in which a technical elite will be like the artisans of medieval times, and transnational corporate CEOs along with international investment bankers will exercise power equivalent to the lords and ladies of feudal times.

▪ October 7–8: The Rockefeller Brothers Fund and the World Bank host a meeting of foundation executives, leaders of environmental NGOs (non-governmental organizations), officers of large multilateral institutions, and others. The meeting is entitled "Building a Constituency for Global Interdependence."

▪ October 23: On "The Charlie Rose Show" on the Public Broadcasting System, Mikhail Gorbachev states: "We are part of the Cosmos. Cosmos is my God. Nature is my God. . . . The future society will be a totally new civilization which will synthesize the experience of Socialism and Capitalism. . . ."

▪ November 16: Richard Barrett, values coordinator for the World Bank, delivers an address to the World Goodwill Symposium. World Goodwill is a service activity of the Lucis Trust, formerly Lucifer Publishing. Barrett's address is published by World Goodwill as an "Occasional Paper," which is one of those World Goodwill defines as "a series of papers by leading servers." And among the authors of "Occasional Papers," World Goodwill lists Gustave Speth (Rhodes Scholar 1964), director of the United Nations Development Program, a position for which he was recommended by President Clinton.

▪ November–December: *Society* publishes "Winners and Losers in the Information Age" by Ian Angell of the London School of Economics and Political Science (established by the Fabian Socialists), in which he proclaims:

> Individuals and companies are setting up large transnational networks that pay absolutely no heed to national boundaries and barriers. . . . Those who wrap themselves in the flag can soon expect to be buried in it. . . . We can expect massive civil unrest and disorder. . . . Governments, like all other organizations, will have to survive economically on the efforts of an elite few—and no nation–state has an automatic right to exist. . . . Governments will have no other choice other than to acquiesce to the will of global enterprise.

> . . . As far as global enterprises are concerned, liberal democracy is an artifact . . . [which] will soon mutate into irrelevancy. It will be merely the means of governing the immobile and dependent social workers. That citizens elect their slave masters makes democracy slavery none the less. . . . The masses will not win in the natural selection for dominance of an increasingly elitist world.

▪ December 9: Secretary of Defense William Perry introduces Communist Chinese defense minister General Chi Hoatian not as "my counterpart" but as "my colleague," even though Chi Hoatian has killed American troops in Korea, and it was he who ordered the tanks into Tiananmen Square where the massacre of Chinese students occurred. General Xu Huizi actually ordered the massacre, and in August of 1997, he will be invited by Secretary Perry into the Pentagon's War Room. This will be followed two months later by the establishment of the U.S.-China Defense Conversion Commission to facilitate technology transfers from the U.S. to China. The U.S. has even permitted China to obtain the most accurate targeting systems for cruise missiles and to buy technology used to build "stealth" aircraft, with some of this technology transfer approved by the U.S. Department of Commerce when Ron Brown (CFR member who was killed) was its Secretary. On September 15, 1998, Defense Secretary William Cohen will sign an agreement with a high-ranking Chinese army official. According to an Associated Press report, the agreement in part "commits their countries to exchange information about how to protect the environment while conducting military operations." Does this mean that while soldiers would be killing other soldiers in a real battle, they must see that no trees, rivers, or endangered species anywhere are harmed?

- December 9–13: World Trade Organization (WTO) Director-General Renato Ruggiero, at the WTO's Singapore Ministerial, says: "We are writing the constitution of a single global economy." And at the June 19, 1997, Common Market Council meeting in Paraguay, he will state:

> The defining events of this new era—and the new century—is globalization. Globalization is about . . . the gradual convergence of our interests, our goals and aspirations, and our perceptions of the world. . . . The great divisions of the last century . . . are slowly fading into history. In their place, we find a new momentum towards a new kind of international order. . . . However ambitious the scope of regionalism, the reality is that we are moving towards an economy of global dimensions . . . as we design the rules of the twenty-first century economy . . . [for] this new economic order. . . . Rule-based global integration will not be a smooth or painless process. . . . The universal rule-based multilateral trading system is rapidly becoming a central pillar of the new international order. . . . The alternative would be a world . . . influenced by economic and political nationalism. In brief, a world moving towards repeating the well-known tragedies of our history.

▪ *Washington Post* columnist E. J. Dionne, Jr. (Rhodes Scholar 1973–75) authors *They Only Look Dead*, in which he claims that the U.S. is not going to the "right," but rather wants a new "progressive" (liberal) tradition. Dionne will also be a Senior Fellow at the Brookings Institute.

▪ *A Reporter's Life* by Walter Cronkite is published, in which he proclaims: "If we are to avoid catastrophe, a system of world order—preferably a system of world government—is mandatory. The proud nations someday will . . . yield up their precious sovereignty."

▪ James Fallows (Rhodes Scholar 1970) becomes editor of *U.S. News and World Report*. He has been editor of *The Washington Monthly* and Washington editor of *The Atlantic*.

1997

▪ January 2: U.N. Secretary-General Kofi Annan calls Maurice Strong and asks him to oversee efforts to reorganize the U.N. Strong is a senior advisor to Annan and a close friend of Vice-President Al Gore, and *The New York Times* has referred to him as the "Custodian of the Planet." Strong has been on the board of directors of the Aspen Institute for Humanistic Studies, a trustee of the Rockefeller Foundation, a senior advisor to World Bank president James Wolfensohn, and he formed the North American Institute to promote the passage of NAFTA. He has also been a member of the Commission on Global Governance, co-chairman of the Council of the World Economic Forum (Davos, Switzerland), chairman of the

World Resources Institute, executive director of the U.N. Environment Program, and Secretary-General of the 1992 U.N. Conference on Environment and Development (Rio Earth Summit). Furthermore, he has been Undersecretary–General of the U.N. six times, and is considered by some U.N. observers to be a strong candidate for the next Secretary-General of the U.N.

In the May 1990 edition of *West* magazine, writer Daniel Wood recounted Strong's description of a novel he was thinking about writing. Strong said:

> What if a small group of these world leaders [at Davos] were to conclude that the principal risk to the earth comes from the actions of the rich countries? . . . In order to save the planet, the group decides: isn't the only hope for the planet that the industrial civilizations collapse? Isn't it our responsibility to bring that about? This group of world leaders form a secret society to bring about an economic collapse. It's February. They're all at Davos. They have positioned themselves in the world's commodity and stock markets. They've engineered, using their access to stock exchanges and computers and gold supplies, a panic. Then, they prevent the world's stock markets from closing. They jam the gears. They hire mercenaries who hold the rest of the world leaders at Davos as hostages. The markets can't close. . . . I probably shouldn't be saying things like this.

Daniel Wood then remarks, "This is not *any* storyteller talking. This is Maurice Strong. He knows these world leaders. . . . He sits at the fulcrum of power. He is in a position to *do it.*"

▪ February 20: Ronnie L. Edelman, Principal Deputy Chief of the Terrorism and Violent Crime Section within the Criminal Division of the U.S. Department of Justice, writes a letter responding to an inquiry regarding the Clinton administration's views on the Second Amendment and handguns. She states:

> The current state of federal law does not recognize that the Second Amendment protects the right of private citizens to possess firearms of any type. Instead, the Second Amendment is deemed to be a collective right belonging to the state, not to an individual.

This means that the Clinton administration believes Americans have no Second Amendment rights as individuals.

▪ September 22: President Clinton delivers an address to the U.N. General Assembly in which he calls for the creation of a permanent international court by the end of the century, and he also says: "The forces of global integration are a great tide, inexorably wearing away the established order of things."

▪ September 24: Rush Limbaugh on his radio program today, when asked why President Clinton supported NAFTA, replies:

> This is the one issue Clinton has, other than welfare reform, where he has just flown in the face of his constituency groups.... There are forces, powerful forces, outside Washington, who are steering this one.

▪ October 1: The U.S. federal government begins operating a directory of all people hired for any full-time or part-time job in the U.S. All employers are required every three months to report all employees' wages. According to a front page article in the September 22 *New York Times*, the directory will not only include the amount of one's income, but also the amount of one's assets and debts.

▪ *Locked in the Cabinet* by Robert Reich is published soon after he leaves the Clinton administration. In this book, he indicates his belief that Federal Reserve Chairman Alan Greenspan thought of him as a type of "Bolshevik."

▪ *One World, Ready or Not* by William Greider is published. In this book, Greider refers to the "governing elites" more than once, and he also refers to Wendell Willkie's 1943 book, *One World*, saying that

> Willkie's postwar [World War II] world order is now . . . eclipsed by a brave new vision for "global convergence" that is far more radical than anything he imagined. . . . The essence of what is forming now is an economic system of interdependence designed to ignore the prerogatives of nations, even the most powerful ones.

Greider is also the author of *Secrets of the Temple: How the Federal Reserve Runs the Country* (1987).

▪ October 17: In an interview with Argentine reporters in Buenos Aires, President Clinton refers to "the globalization of our economy," and he says:

> What I'm trying to do is to promote a process of reorganization of the world so that human beings are organized in a way that takes advantage of the new opportunities of this era. . . . And if we can prove that you can merge integrated economies and integrated democracies, then we'll be more likely to build a global system of this kind.

▪ November 14: Concerning the crisis when Saddam Hussein expels U.N. weapons inspectors, President Clinton declares: "Instead of complying with the unequivocal will of the international community, Saddam chose . . . to defy the United Nations." At about the same time, Joint Chiefs of Staff chairman General Henry H. Shelton calls the redeployment of U.S. ships to the Persian Gulf "a prudent measure to demonstrate how seriously the U.S. takes this challenge to the authority of the U.N."

▪ December 12: Former British prime minister Margaret Thatcher delivers an address at the Heritage Foundation's twenty-fifth anniversary celebration, in which she asserts that

> today's international policy makers' . . . short-term goal is to subordinate American and other national sovereignties to multilateral authorities; their long-term goal, one suspects, is to establish the U.N. as a kind of embryo world government.

1998

- January 27: In President Clinton's State of the Union address, he remarks:

> It's long past time to make good on our debt to the United Nations. . . . In this new era, our freedom and independence are actually enriched, not impoverished, by our increasing interdependence with other nations. . . . As we move into . . . a global economy, a truly new world . . . America must . . . stand against the poisoned appeals of extreme nationalism.

Is "independence enriched by increasing interdependence" an example of Orwellian "Newspeak"? President Clinton also says in this address:

> We have moved past the sterile debate between those who say government is the enemy and those who say government is the answer. My fellow Americans, we have found a third way.

"The Third Way" has been a theme of British Prime Minister Tony Blair, who is a vice-president of Socialist International. Sweden was perhaps the original "third way," as American journalist Marquis Childs in 1937 wrote *Sweden: The Middle Way,* which described their socialistic compromise between capitalism and communism.

Jean-Francois Revel is a First Endorser of Planetary Citizens, and in his 1992 book, *Democracy Against Itself,* one reads:

> With very few exceptions outside the Soviet sphere, such as the Allende experiment in Chile, the "third way" only lived on paper. With Gorbachev, it was given an empirical test on a large scale. . . . Even the conservatives in the West thought this third way was possible, since Reagan, Bush, Kohl, Andreotti, and Thatcher were among the new general secretary's warmest supporters.

The eventual goal of the power elite is a synthesis of capitalism and communism into a World Socialist Government.

▪ January 29: Speaking at the National Defense University, President Clinton states that "Saddam [Hussein] . . . should comply with the . . . will of the United Nations." Should one infer from this that President Clinton believes that all nations, including the United States, should comply with the will of the United Nations?

▪ February 5: When the subject of possibly removing Saddam Hussein from power arises, President Clinton states "that is not what the U.N. has authorized us to do."

▪ February 24: Bruno Giussani writing for *The New York Times* states:

> A massive telecommunications interception network operates within Europe and, according to a new study, . . . "targets the telephone, fax, and e-mail messages of private citizens, politicians, trade unionists, and companies alike." The report says that the network has the ability to tap into almost all international telecommunications as well as parts of domestic phone traffic and is apparently operated by intelligence agencies without any mechanism of democratic control. The network, dubbed Echelon, is described in a new study by the European Parliament titled "An Appraisal of Technologies of Political Control." . . . The report paints a frightening picture of an Orwellian world. . . . Cameras used for traffic monitoring can easily be adapted to security surveillance. . . . The main actor appears to be the United States National Security Agency. "Within Europe, all e-mail, telephone, and fax communications are routinely intercepted by the NSA," the report charges. . . . There is a pressing need to determine the extent to which these new technologies are about political and social control rather than citizen protection, the report says.

▪ March 2: Brian Williams of MSNBC asks, "How do you, John McCain, as a member of the Senate, go along with ceding U.S. authority to the U.N. [regarding Iraq]?" To which Senator McCain replies: "I worry about it a lot. It reminds me of the black helicopter crowd that claimed we have lost our national sovereignty. . . . I wouldn't have allowed this kind of scenario to transpire."

▪ March 3: *The Philadelphia Inquirer* publishes an "Opinion" which states:

> If there is going to be a shortage of bright, well-educated people, corporations will pay a premium to get them—even import them from overseas. They will then use these geniuses to design production systems that can be run by idiots, whom they will pay as little as possible to make up the difference.

This describes the future techno-feudal society, in which the power elite will have labor serfs or machine serfs, as predicted by W. J. Ghent in 1902 (see excerpts from Ghent's article in *The Independent,* April 3, 1902, on page 221 of this book).

▪ March 26: President Clinton in an address to the Parliament of South Africa states that "we are still bedeviled by notions that our . . . religious differences are somehow more important than our common humanity."

▪ April 27: *Time* magazine, in an article about digital cash crossing national boundaries, states:

> A single electronic card like this [picture of an "Omnicard"] may replace everything in your wallet, including . . . your ID cards. . . . [In the] future, non-conspiracists could consolidate pertinent info (vital

> health data, etc.) in one place. . . . You can send money (to your daughter) over the Internet encoded in an E-mail instead of sending a check. . . . Your daughter can store the money any way she wants . . . even (in the not too distant future) on a chip implanted under her skin.

- May 5: *The New York Times* publishes "The New World Order" by A. M. Rosenthal, in which he writes:

> The U.S., its democratic allies and major dictatorships are rapidly building a new world order. . . . The U.S. gets to sell strategic material to China, offering as an extra a visit by the U.S. President to honor the Communist leaders and expand their power and political life span. Religious and political mavericks in the totalitarian partners of the new world order get prison, or death, often both. The press of the democracies gets to write about the growth of order in the new order. Other citizens of the democracies get to say costs of imported goods are down, how nice. Americans and Europeans may come to object for political or moral reasons, or because the new world order may after all cost them their jobs. . . .

- June 12: *USA Today* publishes an article headlined "Automaker's New World Order," in which one reads that

> General Motors is opening five new plants in Argentina, Poland, China, Thailand, and Brazil. . . . GM is considering closing its largest car factory in North

> America. . . . Says GM Vice-President Donald Hackworth, "We have to compete in this marketplace. Consumers don't care about 'America First' or 'America Last.' Consumers do whatever they want to do." That's a chilling attitude, the United Auto Workers say, one that leads to U.S. becoming expendable. "If we don't stop them," says worker Willie North, walking the picket line, "we won't be here."

▪ June 29: President Clinton speaking to students and the community of Beijing University remarks: "In the twenty-first century your generation must also lead the challenge of an international financial system that has no respect for national borders."

▪ July 1: *The New York Post* publishes an article by Pat Buchanan, who refers to Ralph Nader asking the CEOs of the one hundred largest U.S. corporations to lead their corporations in the pledge of allegiance to the flag of the U.S. at their next shareholders' meetings. Many of them refused, with Kodak, for example, saying it must "maintain a global perspective to compete effectively in a global economy." Buchanan responds:

> American taxpayers guarantee the Export-Import Bank loans of these companies; we bail out their investments via the International Monetary Fund; the U.S. Marines have been sent to protect their property; and U.S. consular officials and presidents have promoted their sales. If they cannot pledge loyalty to America, why should Americans be loyal to them?

▪ July 8: The Associated Press files a story with *The New York Times* about U.S. Supreme Court Justices in Brussels, Belgium. CFR member and Supreme Court Justice Stephen Breyer is quoted as saying: "Why should people in Brussels be telling us what to do? That sounds like people in Tulsa asking, 'Why should Washington tell us what to do?'" And CFR member and Supreme Court Justice Sandra Day O'Connor is reported as saying:

> In the next century, we are going to want to draw upon judgments from other jurisdictions. We are going to be more inclined to look at the decisions of that [European] court . . . and perhaps use them and cite them. . . . We are going to see in the next century a considerable amount of litigation coming out of these [international] treaties.

▪ July 20: On the front page of *The New York Times*, reporter Sheryl Stolberg writes:

> As legislation that would protect patient privacy languishes in Congress, the Clinton Administration is quietly laying plans to assign every American a "unique health identifier," a computer code that could be used to create a national database that would track every citizen's medical history from cradle to grave.

▪ July 25–31: Members of the Association to Unite the Democracies (AUD, begun as Union Now by Rhodes Scholar Clarence Streit) from Europe and America meet at The Hague, The Netherlands, and draft "The Constitution for a Union of Democracies" for a transnational federal government. AUD Advisory Board member Henry Luce III then makes a matching donation of twenty-five thousand dollars to AUD's "Campaign for International Federalism." Luce has been publisher of *Time* and *Fortune* magazines, as well as director of Time-Warner Inc. (1989–96), and a member of the Pilgrims Club (U.S.).

▪ September 11: The Starr Report is presented to Congress, and it describes evidence of possibly impeachable offenses (e.g., perjury before a Grand Jury) by President Clinton. The president, however, insists that he has not committed perjury because he does not consider "having sexual relations" to include oral sex. This reminds one of Lewis Carroll's (member of the Society for Psychical Research) character "Humpty Dumpty" in *Through the Looking Glass.* Humpty Dumpty represents either the current political leader of the day or the power behind the leader. He is precariously balanced upon a wall, yet he believes "there's no chance of" his falling. Humpty Dumpty also believes that a word "means just what I choose it to mean" (e.g., having sex does not include oral sex), and he feels "the question is, which is to be master."

President Clinton's lawyer is David E. Kendall (Rhodes Scholar 1966), who attended Yale Law School at the same time as did Bill Clinton. Kendall also taught law at Georgetown University (from which Bill Clinton graduated in 1968), and he was a law clerk for Supreme Court Justice Byron White (Rhodes Scholar 1938), who likewise graduated from Yale Law School.

Polls show a large majority of Americans believe President Clinton should not resign or be impeached even if he has committed perjury. This raises the important question of what has happened to Americans' values. How can any president tell the Justice Department, the Attorney–General, and the federal courts to prosecute perjurers to the fullest extent of the law but exempt himself?

▪ September 27: *The Washington Post* reports that

> Half an hour after her husband's grand jury testimony began airing on television, Hillary Rodham Clinton was discussing third way politics at the New York University Law School. The discussion was later joined by Clinton, [British Prime Minister Tony] Blair, Italian Prime Minister Romano Prodi, and Bulgarian President Petar Stoyanov."

Anthony Giddens, director of the London School of Economics, also participated. He has recently published a new book on "The Third Way," and in *The Washington Post* article he is quoted as saying:

> The third way agenda, to which Bill and Hillary Clinton have made a fundamental contribution, is the new agenda for our time. Third way politics will dominate the next twenty to thirty years. . . . We are talking about a very fundamental paradigm shift in politics here today.

▪ September/October: *The Humanist* publishes "Beyond Humanist Manifesto II" by Paul Kurtz, who drafted *Hu-*

manist Manifesto II (1973), which he says "prophesied that the twenty-first century could become the humanist century." Kurtz further states that "we need to transcend the hide-bound, archaic religious dogmas of the past," and he offers suggestions about what should be included in a third *Humanist Manifesto.* Kurtz declares that the

> challenge is to develop a new global ethics that transcends our chauvinistic, nationalistic . . . perspectives of the past. . . . Many humanists have argued that we should develop an international system of taxation. . . . It is essential that nation-states transfer some of their sovereignty to a world body. This latter proposal will no doubt engender extreme opposition from conservative nationlists like Senator Jesse Helms. . . . A *new* World Federal Constitution should be concerned with our common and interdependent human interests. . . . Humanists reiterate today, as in the past, that no divine power will rescue us. We are responsible for our own destiny.

▪ October 12: Vice-President Al Gore announces his "Declaration of Interdependence" regarding global technology and telecommunications. There are five steps involved, one of which is the creation of a "global knowledge network" specializing in the delivery of services such as education, health care, and "sustainable development" (e.g., environmental correctness).

▪ October 14: *Investor's Business Daily* publishes "Is Congress Missing in Action?" by Brian Mitchell, in which he says that University of Virginia professor of international law Robert F. Turner (who also teaches at the Naval War College)

> argues the U.S. surrendered its right to wage aggressive war when it joined the United Nations. In exchange, other countries gave up the same right. "I think that's a wonderful thing," Turner said. "We've given up our sovereignty, as the conservatives like to say. . . . Military officers ask, 'Are we in a state of war?' I tell them, 'That is no longer the proper paradigm. What you need to ask is, Is this a situation in which it is lawful under international law to use lethal force.'"

▪ November 12: "ABC News" announces that the Global Warming Treaty is signed by Peter Burleigh, the chief U.S. representative at the U.N. Under the pact, called the Kyoto Protocol, industrial nations must find ways to cut heat-trapping emissions from burning fossil fuels that are believed to cause global warming by an average of 5.2 percent below 1990 levels in the period 2008 to 2012. On December 14, 1997, U.S. Senator Chuck Hagel, just back from the U.N. Global Warming Conference in Kyoto, Japan, appeared on CBS' "Face the Nation," and warned:

> The consequences of the actions that are taken, and if in fact we move forward and ratify this Treaty on Global Warming, are about our jobs, our economic future, our economic growth, international competitiveness, national sovereignty. For example, for the first time in the history of America, we would be allowing a U.N.

bureaucracy to come in and administer and enforce shutdowns of industries, businesses, farmers.

▪ November 30: Deutsche Bank in Frankfurt, Germany, formally announces its plan for a $10.1 billion takeover of the Bankers Trust Corporation in the U.S., and indicates that "most of the power will remain in Frankfurt" (*The New York Times,* December 1, 1998). Along similar lines, British Petroleum announced on August 11 that it was buying Amoco.

▪ December 19: The U.S. House of Representatives votes to impeach President Clinton by a vote of 228 to 206 on the charge of committing perjury before a Grand Jury, and by a vote of 221 to 212 on the charge of obstruction of justice. This historic vote constitutionally results in a trial of President Clinton on those charges in the U.S. Senate, and that begins in January 1999. President Clinton is still confident that sixty-seven senators (the required minimum for conviction) will not vote to convict him on those charges, and he also refuses to resign.

▪ December 21: Congressman Bob Barr is one of the members of the U.S. House of Representatives who will prosecute the case against President Clinton in the U.S. Senate. On today's Rush Limbaugh program, he states regarding President Clinton:

> You have here a man whose sole purpose in being is to gain power and to hold on to power, both he and Hillary [Clinton], and that's what they're engaged in.

> They will do absolutely anything—legal, illegal, moral, immoral—in order to remain in power. . . . That's what we're witnessing here. We're witnessing absolute power, absolutely corrupting.

1999

▪ January 1: The "Euro," the combined currency of the European Common Market, goes into effect in international trading and will account for about one-fifth of the world's economic output and trade.

▪ January 8: President Clinton delivers a speech to the Detroit Economic Club, in which he describes what he believes "the role of government" should be. He states:

> Some have called this political philosophy "the third way." It has modernized progressive political parties and brought them to power throughout the industrial world. Here in America it has led us, I believe, to a new consensus, making the vital center once again a source of energy, action and progress. That, I believe, is the only way for any advanced industrial nation to thrive in the new global economy.

▪ May 17–19: The Centennial World Peace Conference is held at The Hague, The Netherlands, with the Program of Action presented by the governments of The Netherlands and the Russian Federation. The Program of Action has been welcomed by the U.N.

▪ July 29–August 1: The World Future Society's 9th General Assembly is held, with sessions on the environment, new technologies, social change, public policy, economics and finance, future methodologies, and more.

▪ December 1–8: The Parliament of the World Religions meets in South Africa "seeking the moral and ethical convergence [common ground] that leads to shared commitment and action."

2000

▪ By this year, radical feminist leader Gloria Steinem stated, "we will, I hope, raise our children to believe in human potential, not God." (*Saturday Review of Education,* February 10, 1973)

▪ By this year, former National Education Association president Catherine Barrett stated:

> Dramatic changes in the way we raise our children are indicated, particularly in terms of schooling. . . . We will need to recognize that the so-called "basic skills," which currently [1973] represent nearly the total effort in elementary schools, will be taught in one-quarter of the present school day. . . . When this happens—and it's near—the teacher can rise to his true calling. More than a dispenser of information, the teacher will be a conveyor of values, a philosopher. . . . We will be agents of change.
>
> —*Saturday Review of Education*, February 10, 1973

▪ December 26: This is the date given at the beginning of

Theodore Brameld's *The Teacher As World Citizen* (actually published in 1974), commemorating Edward Bellamy's *Looking Backward.* Writing as if it is December 26, 2000 A.D., leading collectivist educator Brameld portrays a World Community of Nations as a transnational government with a World Order Party based on the ideals of "humanistic socialism," and with a peacekeeping force of fifty thousand men and women. He says it is the Age of Eros and sexual freedom, and children are reared in *kibbutzim* from nursery through high school under the auspices of a World Education Authority. In the mid-1960s Brameld had declared that national sovereignty was outmoded and dangerous, and he called for world government. At about that same time, Brameld was invited by the U.S. Commissioner of Education to serve on a committee to plan the future of education in the U.S.

2010

▪ By this year, according to strategic futurist Charles W. Taylor's *A World 2010: A New Order of Nations* (published in 1992 by the Strategic Studies Institute of the U.S. Army War College), "the new order of nations almost certainly will [have] evolved gradually into a world economy." He also has advocated a national educational system, policy, and programs "that would be most beneficial for the nation and prepare the people best for the work environment of the world of 2010."

2018

▪ Around this year, according to *The Economist* (January 9, 1988), people should

> pencil in the phoenix . . . and welcome it when it comes. . . . There would be no such thing . . . as a national monetary policy. The world phoenix [international monetary unit or coin] supply would be fixed by a new central bank, descended perhaps from the IMF. The world inflation rate—and hence, within narrow margins, each national inflation rate—would be in its charge. . . . This means a big loss of economic sovereignty.

2025

▪ By this year, according to Dr. Christopher Winter (research group leader at British Telecom's Laboratories), a computer chip (implanted behind the eye) can record a person's every sensation, which can then be played back by a computer (*Business Week*, August 5, 1996).

▪ By this year, according to Alice Bailey, the "outer form" of the "World Federation of Nations" will be "taking rapid shape." She stated this in her pamphlet, "The Next Three Years (1934–1935–1936)," and she further remarked concerning this World Federation of Nations "taking rapid shape by 2025" that one should

> not infer by this that we shall have a perfected world religion and a complete community of nations. Not so rapidly does nature move, but the vision and the idea will be universally recognized, universally desired, and generally worked for. When these conditions exist, nothing can stop the appearance of the ultimate physical form. . . . Approximately four hun-

> dred men and women are working consciously with the Plan.

Bailey was probably the leading occultist of the first half of the 1900s, and she often wrote about the need for a "new world order" with "points of light" connected to "service." Her works were originally published by Lucifer Publishing, later known as Lucis Trust, which has maintained the U.N.'s "meditation room."

Conclusion

It has not been the purpose of this book to suggest that every single Rhodes Scholar (or member of some organization or society) has been plotting to take over the world, for they have not. However, to ignore the quotations and activities of the globalists mentioned on the preceding pages would also be folly, for we have been and are being internationalized into a New World Order.

That we are being internationalized whether or not we like it is evident from the fact that Congress had approved a measure requiring that by 1995, all federal highway signs be in metric. This is despite Americans' dislike of conversion to metric measurements expressed several years ago, but it is necessary if we are to be made to conform to the system of measurement used by most other nations.

Before the elitist world-planners can internationalize everything into the New World Order socialist world government, however, key aspects of life in each country must first be nationalized. That is why in the United States today there is a movement toward such things as national education standards, national service, a national health plan, and a national police force.

In *American Museum* (July 1792), Philip Freneau tried to warn the American people in what was their young Republic about what a power elite might try to do. He said the power elite would emphasize the *limitations* of the Republic's *Constitution.* The "grand nostrum" of Freneau's outline of the power elite's possible plan was the creation of *debt* "made as big as possible, as perpetual as possible, in as few hands as possible," and as complicated as possible. He then said, "A great debt will require great taxes. . . . Money will be put under the direction of government, and government under the direction of money." Freneau then indicated that the power elite would give a popular name, such as "the general welfare," to the usurped power so that those opposing the elite could be negatively labeled as "opposing the general welfare" of the people. And lastly, Freneau noted that those warning about the elite's attempt to seize power would themselves be labeled as "enemies to the established government." He declared that this charge would "be reiterated and reverberated till at last such confusion and uncertainty be produced that the people, being not able to find out where the truth lies, withdraw their attention from the contest."

Years later, Alexis DeTocqueville in *Democracy in America* (1840) expressed his concerns regarding potential despotisms as follows:

> Above this race of men stands an immense and tutelary power, which takes upon itself alone to secure

> their gratifications and to watch over their fate. . . . After having thus successively taken each member of the community in its powerful grasp and fashioned him at will, the supreme power then extends its arm over the whole community. . . . The will of man is not shattered, but softened, bent, and guided. . . . It does not tyrannize, but it compresses, enervates, extinguishes, and stupefies a people, till each nation is reduced to nothing better than a flock of timid and industrious animals, of which the government is the shepherd.

At the national level, this conditioning of the public might be brought about via certain crises, such as a high rate of crime. For the sake of peace and security, people may be willing to give up certain of their freedoms to some extent.

In that regard, on ABC's "20/20" (September 1, 1995), Hugh Downs said, "Big Brother has finally arrived. . . . People are being watched from cameras half-a-mile away." And reporter Lynn Sher then explained that

> surveillance cameras are being used to patrol entire [more than one hundred] British communities. . . . These are the omnipresent eyes of the law. . . . It's the Big Brother issue. . . . A police chief in Scotland says: "When crime and when disorder and when people's fears become so acute that they are crying out for something to be done about it, then perhaps they have to give up just a little bit more of [their] freedoms in order to counteract it."

Although people nationally and internationally want peace and safety, remember that First Thessalonians 5:3 states: "For when they shall say, Peace and safety; then sudden destruction cometh upon them, . . . and they shall not escape."

Fabian Socialist H.G. Wells said many years ago that the final coming of the planned world socialist government would in all likelihood occur very quickly. And remember that in his book *The Shape of Things to Come* (1933) he foretold that although the world government "had been plainly coming for some years, although it had been endlessly feared and murmured against, it found no opposition prepared anywhere." The existence of the power elite would finally be acknowledged and its influence accepted. As Orwell wrote in *1984,* they "will come to love Big Brother."

What the power elite probably has in mind is the synthesizing of Western capitalism and Eastern communism into a World Socialist Government. Hong Kong (formerly capitalist) taken over by China (communist) may be the model for this synthesis. The World Socialist Government will be described as necessary to manage the global economy, thereby avoiding international economic crises like those of the past. Relevant to this are President Clinton's remarks to the Council on Foreign Relations in New York City on September 14, 1998, where he referred to international "economic turmoil," to Russia's "economic crisis," and to the international "currency crisis." He also referred to "building a global economic system," and further stated: "No nation, rich or poor, democratic or authoritarian, can escape the fundamental economic imperatives of the global market. . . ." There has even been speculation that the economic hardships caused by the year A.D. 2000 (Y2K) computer problems may provide the power elite with the excuse they are looking for to claim the need for world government.

A good deal has been said about the men and the money moving us toward the New World Order, but the methods being used are also important. They include national and international banking and corporate mergers (which allow downsizing and worker layoffs); public–private partnerships; consciousness-changing techniques via religion, arts, education, music, media, etc.; facilitated consensus in T-groups, conferences, forums, summits, and other meetings via Delphi and other techniques; regionalism; Total Quality Management (e.g., managing "human capital" or "human resources" via the International Standardization Organization Reference Model); convergence (e.g., to the "Third Way") by dialectical materialistic processes; and networking (refer to *The Age of Networking: Organizing Principles for the 21st Century* by Jessica Lipnack and Jeffrey Stamps, who met while students at Oxford University in 1968 where Jeffrey met Bill Clinton and saw his "little black address book," which Clinton kept for future political reference).

If the World Socialist Government comes into existence, there will be no escaping it,[29] and it will be corrupt, because as Lord Acton wrote to Bishop Creighton on April 5, 1887: "Power tends to corrupt and absolute power corrupts absolutely."

Biblical prophecy is relevant here in the following sense. Revelation 13:18 refers to the number of the Beast as 666. The key to understanding this may be in First Kings 10:14 and Second Chronicles 9:13, which indicate 666 was the weight of talents of gold that was brought each year to Solomon, who would worship Astarte, the goddess of the Sidonians. In Benjamin Disraeli's *Coningsby: or the New Generation* (1844), the key character is Sidonia, who says: "So you see, my dear Coningsby, that the world is governed by very different personages from what is imagined by those who are not behind the scenes."

In Revelation, the final battle takes place at Armageddon. This is, in a worldly sense, the final battle for world control, for who will control the world government, which could be brought about through world trade. This is because in Solomon's time, he fortified Gezer, Hazor, and Megiddo. The Har (Mount) of Megiddo would be called Armageddon, and through this fortification, Solomon controlled the Via Maris and world trade, thereby controlling the world of his day.

In a spiritual sense, Astarte was the Phoenician goddess Ashteroth, the female half of Baal (New Agers refer to a future of androgyny or of yin-yang). Human babies were sacrificed to Baal (like abortions today) under Ahab, who had married Jezebel, the daughter of the Sidonian (Phoenician) king, Ethbaal. But like the battle between the God of Elijah and the prophets of the Phoenicians' Baal during Ahab's time, Baal (Satan) symbolically rises like the Phoenix from the ashes to do battle with the actually-risen Lord, Jesus Christ, Who is victorious.

Jesus said that the signs of the end times could be

readily discernible. They may, indeed, be evident before our very eyes today. Just a few years ago, who would have imagined that an American president could veto a ban on partial-birth abortions (where a baby's brains are literally sucked out as he or she is being born), and the veto would be upheld? Even the pro-choice American Medical Association has declared such abortions are never necessary, yet there was no overriding outrage on the part of the American public regarding the president's and Congress' action. This clearly demonstrates the moral lethargy and degeneration of so many of the American people today.

One purpose in writing *Secret Records Revealed* is with the hope and fervent prayer that it will alert and awaken to the truth many of America's prodigal souls, so that they will return to the foundations upon which this nation was built. Much like the "prodigal son" in *The Holy Bible*, too many no longer love and serve the Father, but have squandered their inheritance, then turning to serve idols, partaking of the fruits which have fallen from the "Ism" Tree (e.g., naturalism, humanism, atheism, materialism, liberalism, socialism, globalism, pantheism, occultism, New Age-ism, or whatever "new thing" that comes along). See Acts 17:16, 21–22 and Isaiah 5:20–21.

Let us hope, however, that the American people arise from their lethargy, and reverse their moral degeneracy, and prove H. G. Wells wrong by resisting the efforts of today's elitist descendants of the French Revolution's "philosopher-kings" who would rule over us.[30] Remember that *The Holy Bible* warns us in Colossians 2:8 to "beware lest any man spoil you through philosophy and vain deceit, after the tradition of men, after the rudiments of the world, and not after Christ."

Over a long period of time, the plan of the "philosopher-kings" was laid out in their secret records. But "it is no secret what God can do" (to quote the well-known Christian song), not only for individuals but for nations, if enough people will turn back to Him in sincere repentance and prayer. And let us hope that this happens before it's too late.

Appendix

This is an alphabetical list of some of the numerous additional Rhodes Scholars (RS) and what they have been doing in the 1990s:

Abbot, Charles (RS 1967)—Rear Admiral, U.S. Navy

Abeln-Touhey, Maura (RS 1977)—vice-president and general counsel for GE Plastics

Adams, Rex (RS 1962)—vice-president of administration for the Mobil Corporation

Agrast, Mark (RS 1978)—senior legislative assistant for Congressman Gerry Studds

Amoss, W. James, III (RS 1969)—editor at the *Times-Picayune* (New Orleans)

Anderson, Betsy (RS 1980)—works for Bell Atlantic

Atkeson, Timothy (RS 1947)—works for the Environmental Law Institute

Badgett, Lee (RS 1961)—provost and dean of faculty of VMI

Baer, George (RS 1957)—professor of strategy at the U.S. Naval War College

Banks, R. Darryl (RS 1972)—a director at the World Resources Institute

Barber, Charles F. (RS 1939)—on the board of directors of various Salomon Brothers funds; has been an assistant U.S. solicitor-general, as well as a member of the CFR and Pilgrims

Bardell, William (RS 1961)—works for Lehman Brothers, international bankers

Barr, Michael (RS 1987)—law clerk for U.S. Supreme Court Justice David Souter

Bartlett, Thomas (RS 1951)—chancellor of the Oregon State System of Higher Education and formerly chancellor of the university systems in Alabama and New York, and in the 1960s and 1970s he was president of the American University in Cairo, Colgate University, and the American Association of Universities

Baskin, Pat, Jr. (RS 1979)—works for Goldman Sachs, international bankers

Blustein, Paul (RS 1973)—correspondent for *The Washington Post,* Tokyo bureau

Bock, David (RS 1967)—managing director of Lehman Brothers, London

Bogan, Willie (RS 1971)—Office of the General Council for Bank of America

Brown, Kenneth (RS 1975)—chairman and CEO of General Electric de Mexico

Bruckner, Donald (RS 1955)—works for *The New York Times*

Bryant, Ralph, III (RS 1960)—senior fellow with the Brookings Institute

Burnett, Howard (RS 1952)—president of Washington and Jefferson College

Calabresi, Guido (RS 1953)—dean of Yale Law School

Campion, Edward (RS 1967)—deputy editor of the *New England Journal of Medicine*

Cannon, Michael (RS 1973)—vice-chancellor and general counsel for Washington University (St. Louis)

Cardinale, Gerald (RS 1989)—works for Goldman Sachs & Co. in Asia

Caudill, Randall (RS 1969)—works for Prudential Securities

Celeste, Richard (RS 1960)—has been governor of Ohio; on the board of trustees for the Carnegie Corporation; a CFR member; and was director of Peace Corps

Clark, Wesley (RS 1966)—commanding general of the 1st Cavalry Division

Cleveland, Sarah (RS 1987)—law clerk for U.S. Supreme Court Justice Harry Blackmun

Coggins, Paul, Jr. (RS 1973)—U.S. Attorney, Dallas

Coldren, Lee (RS 1964)—with the U.S. Foreign Service

Cook, W. Bruce (RS 1957)—vice-president and controller for the Exxon Corporation, Texas

Cooper, James H. S. (RS 1975)—member of Congress for Tennessee

Cowen, Penelope (RS 1984)—private sector development specialist with the World Bank

Crovitz, L. Gordon (RS 1980)—editor of the *Far Eastern Economic Review*

Crowley, William (RS 1979)—executive director of Goldman Sachs International Ltd., London

Davis, Jerome (RS 1971)—president of Cummins Power Generation Inc. of Cummings Engine Co.

DiBona, Charles (RS 1957)—president of the American Petroleum Institute

Doty, James (RS 1962)—with Baker and Botts, Attorneys (Baker refers to President Bush's chief of staff, James Baker)

Early, Stewart (RS 1966)—manager, Planning and Economics, Amoco Pipeline Co.

Ellison, Keith (RS 1972)—partner in Baker & Botts, Attorneys (Houston)

Engle, James B. (RS 1947)—foreign affairs consultant who has been a diplomat to many nations; was with the National Security Council

Feingold, Russell (RS 1975)—United States Senator from Wisconsin

Finegold, David (RS 1985)—works for the Rand Corporation

Fletcher, Richard (RS 1964)—economist with the Inter-American Development Bank

Fornell, Eric (RS 1978)—vice-president of Goldman Sachs & Co., New York

Foulon, Mark (RS 1978)—staff member of U.S. Senator Bill Bradley

Frank, Grady (RS 1930)—military intelligence, retired

Frechtling, Louis (RS 1936)—Department of State, retired

Frohnmayer, David (RS 1962)—president of the University of Oregon

Galpin, Timothy (RS 1982)—Lt. Commander, U.S. Navy

Gardner, James R. (RS 1937)—intelligence officer, Department of State, retired

Gellman, Barton (RS 1982)—staff writer for *The Washington Post*

Gerdine, Leigh (RS 1938)—president emeritus of Webster University

Gerrity, Thomas (RS 1964)—dean of the Wharton School, University of Pennsylvania

Gerson, Elliot (RS 1974)—American secretary of the Rhodes Scholarship Trust (1998); president of Travelers Insurance Company; has also worked for the Department of Defense; was a law clerk for U.S. Supreme Court Justice Potter Stewart; CFR member; was director of the Connecticut Civil Liberties Union

Giard, George, Jr. (RS 1960)—chairman of the board and CEO for Presidio Oil Company

Gifford, Prosser (RS 1951)—director of Scholarly Programs for the Library of Congress

Gillette, Michael (RS 1959)—director of the G7 Support Implementation Group, Russian Federation, the U.S. Embassy in Moscow

Gong, Gerrit (RS 1977)—director of the Asian studies program at the Center for Strategic and International Studies

Gorenflo, Mark (RS 1983)—Lt. Commander, U.S. Navy

Graves, Howard (RS 1961)—Lt. General, U.S. Army; superintendent of the U.S. Military Academy at West Point

Grewe, Barbara (RS 1978)—Assistant U.S. Attorney, District of Columbia

Haass, Richard (RS 1973)—senior associate with the Carnegie Endowment for International Peace, who worked for the State Department during the Reagan administration

Hagerott, Mark (RS 1983)—Lt. Commander, U.S. Navy

Halter, William (RS 1983)—Federal Office of Management and Budget

Hamachek, Ross (RS 1964)—vice-president of planning and development for *The Washington Post* Co.

Harrison, Robert (RS 1976)—vice-president of investment banking for Goldman Sachs & Co., New York

Haverkamp, Jennifer (RS 1979)—director for environmental policy, Office of the U.S. Trade Representative

Heineman, Ben W., Jr. (RS 1965)—general counsel for the General Electric Co.

Hester, James (RS 1947)—president of the Harry Frank Guggenheim Foundation

Himes, James (RS 1988)—works for Goldman Sachs, international bankers, in New York

Hosmer, Bradley (RS 1959)—Lt. General, U.S. Air Force

Hughes, Thomas (RS 1947)—president emeritus of the Carnegie Endowment for International Peace

Hughston, Lane P. (RS 1972)—works for Merrill Lynch International, London

Jacobson, Raymond (RS 1948)—chairman of the CXR Corporation

Jehl, Douglas (RS 1984)—columnist for *The New York Times*

Johnson, Robbin (RS 1968)—works for Cargill Inc.

Jones, Boisefeuillet, Jr. (RS 1968)—vice-president and counsel of *The Washington Post*

Killefer, Tom (RS 1939)—chairman emeritus of U.S. Trust Co. of New York

Kirkwood, Murray (RS 1934)—vice-president of ITT World Communications Inc., retired

Krislov, Marvin (RS 1983)—Office of Counsel to the President

Kristof, Nicholas (RS 1981)—foreign correspondent for *The New York Times*

Lackritz, Marc (RS 1969)—president of the Securities Industry Association

Lambert, Thomas, Jr. (RS 1936)—distinguished professor of Suffolk University Law School, Boston; editor-in-chief emeritus of the Association of Trial Lawyers of America

Lassila, Kathrin (RS 1982)—editor of *The American Journal* of the Natural Resources Defense Council

Lawrence, Gary (RS 1980)—investment banker with Goldman Sachs & Co., New York

Lee, Ronald (RS 1980)—general counsel for the National Security Agency

Lemoyne, James (RS 1975)—bureau chief of *The New York Times,* El Salvador

Liu, Goodwin (RS 1991)—works for the Corporation for National Service

Long, Robert, Jr. (RS 1980)—Office of the Solicitor General, U.S. Department of Justice

MacVicar, R. W. (RS 1939)—president emeritus of Oregon State University

Mahoney, Sean (RS 1984)—vice-president of investment banking for Goldman Sachs & Co., New York

Manget, Fred (RS 1973)—general counsel for the CIA

Maynes, Charles, Jr. (RS 1960)—editor of *Foreign Policy*

McFarland, Laurel (RS 1984)—economist with the Brookings Institution

McGuire, Martin (RS 1955)—Clifford S. Heinz Professor for the Economics of Global Peace and Security, UC-Irvine

McKnight, H. Brent (RS 1974)—United States magistrate judge, Charlotte, NC

McManus, Jason (RS 1958)—editor-in-chief of Time-Warner Inc.

McQuade, Lawrence (RS 1950)—vice-chairman of mutual fund management of Prudential Securities, Inc.

Mendenhall, Thomas (RS 1933)—president emeritus of Smith College

Min, Nancy-Ann (RS 1979)—associate director of the Federal Office of Management and Budget, who was named as a future leader of America in *Time* (December 5, 1994)

Monroe, Hunter (RS 1984)—works for the International Monetary Fund

Moose, James (RS 1961)—works for the World Bank

Muller, Stevens (RS 1949)—president emeritus of the Johns Hopkins University

Murphy, Ewell, Jr. (RS 1948)—partner in Baker & Botts, Attorneys, Houston

Muscatine, Alison (RS 1977)—a speechwriter for Hillary Clinton

Nason, John (RS 1928)—president emeritus of Carleton College

Nolte, Richard (RS 1947)—on the board of directors of the Fund for Peace; a CFR member; has been ambassador to Egypt and assistant director of humanities for the Rockefeller Foundation

O'Flaherty, J. Daniel (RS 1965)—vice-president and secretary of the National Foreign Trade Council, Inc.; executive director of the U.S.-South Africa Business Council

Ooms, Van Doorn (RS 1956)—senior vice-president of the Committee for Economic Development

O'Toole, James (RS 1966)—senior fellow with the Aspen Institute for Humanistic Studies

Page, John, Jr. (RS 1971)—works for the World Bank

Parker, W. Carey (RS 1956)—legislative assistant to U.S. Sen. Edward Kennedy

Peck, Bobby, Jr. (RS 1988)—works for the Perot Group

Pelz, Edward (RS 1939)—personnel executive for *The New York Times*, retired

Pfeiffer, Steven (RS 1969)—partner with the law firm of Fulbright & Jaworski

Pint, Ellen (RS 1982)—works for the Rand Corporation

Pirie, Robert, Jr. (RS 1956)—Assistant Secretary to the Navy (Installations and Environment)

Poliakoff, Michael (RS 1975)—program officer with the Division of Research Programs of the National Endowment for the Humanities

Ponsor, Michael (RS 1969)—U.S. District Court judge, Massachusetts

Posvar, Wesley (RS 1948)—president emeritus of the University of Pittsburgh

Price, John (RS 1960)—managing director of Chemical Bank, New York City

Radtke, Robert (RS 1987)—vice-president of Business Council for the United Nations

Rea, Graeme (RS 1959)—administration director for IMF

Reinecke, Thomas (RS 1968)—physicist with the Naval Research Laboratory

Ritch, John, III (RS 1965)—U.S. Ambassador to the United Nations in Vienna

Rodrick, Theodore (RS 1960)—program manager for TRW Space and Defense, retired

Roe, David (RS 1969)—senior attorney with the Environmental Defense Fund

Rosenblatt, Lief (RS 1974)—managing director of Soros Fund Management

Rosenheim, Andrew (RS 1977)—director of electronic publishing for Oxford University Press

Sancton, Thomas (RS 1971)—senior editor with *Time*

Sewall, John (RS 1958)—vice-director of the Institute for National Strategic Studies at the National Defense University; Major General, U.S. Army, retired

Shannon, Edgar, Jr. (RS 1947)—president emeritus of the University of Virginia

Shea, Patrick (RS 1970)—director of the U.S. Bureau of Land Management

Shepherd, Robert (RS 1951)—member of the GATT Textiles Surveillance Body, Geneva, Switzerland

Sherwood, Elizabeth (RS 1981)—Deputy Assistant Secretary of Defense at the Pentagon

Sibley, Alden (RS 1933)—Major General, U.S. Army, retired; Economic Development Council of New York City, retired; Champion International Corporation, retired

Sieverts, Frank (RS 1955)—works for the U.S. Senate Foreign Relations Committee

Stamas, Stephen (RS 1953)—chairman of the New York Philharmonic; has been a vice-president of Exxon

Stromberg, Jackson (RS 1958)—senior vice-president of Bechtel Group, Inc.; president of Bechtel Financing Services

Stromseth, Jane (RS 1978)—associate professor at Georgetown University Law Center

Suits, Christopher (RS 1981)—director of Lehman Brothers International, London

Sullivan, John, Jr. (RS 1962)—policy analyst with McDonnell Douglas Corporation

Teitelbaum, Michael (RS 1966)—program officer with the Alfred P. Sloan Foundation

Thompson, James (RS 1951)—assistant to the mayor of Boise, Idaho; Lt. General, U.S. Army, retired

Thompson, Richard (RS 1955)—coordinator for professional issues, American Foreign Service Association

Timmons, Benson, III (RS 1938)—ambassador, retired

Tu, Lawrence (RS 1976)—executive director and general counsel for Goldman Sachs (Asia) Ltd., Hong Kong

Turpin, William (RS 1947)—economics professor; Foreign Service officer, retired

Van De Krol, Ronald (RS 1980)—Netherlands correspondent for the *Financial Times* (London)

Vaughn, William (RS 1925)—chairman of Eastman Kodak Company, retired

Vesser, Dale (RS 1954)—Deputy Assistant Secretary of Defense (Resources and Plans); Lt. General, U.S. Army, retired

Von Kaenel, Howard (RS 1969)—Deputy Undersecretary of Defense (Policy); Brigadier General, U.S. Army, retired

Wagenseil, Harris (RS 1967)—vice-president of supply and maintenance operations for Union Pacific Railroad

Walker, Darrell (RS 1976)—senior vice-president of Columbia Pictures, Columbia Studios

Westbrook, Sam, III (RS 1963)—vice-president and general manager of the military products unit of Abex NWL Aerospace; Brigadier General, U.S. Air Force, retired

Westling, Jon (RS 1964)—executive vice-president and provost of Boston University

Williams, Mark (RS 1973)—manager of staff development for Shell Oil Company, Houston

Willkie, Wendell (RS 1973)—visiting fellow at the American Enterprise Institute

Wilson, John (RS 1953)—president of Washington and Lee University

Wood, D. Joseph (RS 1963)—vice-president of the World Bank for the South Asia region

■ ■ ■ ■ ■

The Independent (April 3, 1902) published *"The Next Step: A Benevolent Feudalism"* by W. J. Ghent (former editor of *The American Fabian*) in which he wrote that the

> . . . coming status . . . will be something in the nature of a Benevolent Feudalism. . . . Group fidelity . . . is already observable. . . . The autocrats . . . will distribute benefits to the degree that makes a tolerant, if not satisfied people. . . . A person of offensive activity may be denied work in every feudal shop and on every feudal farm from one end of the country to the other. . . . His actions will be promptly communicated to the banded autocracy of dukes, earls and marquises of industries. . . . The individual security of place and livelihood of its members will then depend on the harmony of their utterances and acts with the wishes of the great nobles; and so long as they rightly fulfill their functions their recompense will be generous. They will be at once the assuagers of popular suspicion and discontent and the providers of moral and intellectual anodynes for the barons. . . . A host of economists, preachers and editors will be ready to show indisputably that the evolution taking place is for the best interests of all. . . . What the barons will most dread will be the collective assertion of the villains at the polls; but this, from experience, they will know to be a thing of no immediate danger. By the putting forward of a hundred irrelevant issues they can hopelessly divide the voters at each election; or, that failing, there is al-

ways to be trusted as a last resort the cry of impending panic. . . . Two divisions of the courtier class are the judges and the politicians. . . . They must satisfy the demands of the multitude, and yet, on the other hand, they must obey the commands from above. . . . The nobles will have attained to complete power, and the motive and operation of Government will have become simply the registering and administering of their collective will. . . . Armed force will, of course be employed to overawe the discontented and to quiet unnecessary turbulence. Unlike the armed forces of the old feudalism, the nominal control will be that of the State. . . . When the new order is in full swing . . . so comprehensive and so exact will be the social and political control that it will be exercised in a constantly widening scope. . . . Peace [and stability] will be the main desideratum. . . . A happy blending of generosity and firmness will characterize all dealings with open discontent. . . . [to] the prevention of discontent . . . the teachings of the schools and colleges, the sermons, the editorials . . . and even the plays at the theaters will be skillfully and persuasively molded.

▪ ▪ ▪ ▪ ▪

Investigative reporter Thomas Lawson in "Frenzied Finance" (*Everybody's Magazine*, August 1904):

> There gather each day, between the hours of eleven and twelve o'clock, all the active men whose efforts make "Standard Oil" what "Standard Oil" is. . . . Reports are presented . . . republics and empires made and unmade. . . . The success of "Standard Oil" is largely due to two things—the loyalty of its members to each other and to "Standard Oil" and the punishment of its enemies. Each member before initiation knows its religion to be reward for friends and extermination of enemies. Once a man is within the magic circle . . . punishment for disloyalty is sure and terrible, and in no corner of the earth can he escape it, nor can any power on earth protect him from it. . . . Every twist and turn in the pedigree and records of Republicans and Democrats are as familiar to (the head of Standard Oil) as the "dope sheets" are to the gambler, for is he not at the receiving end of the greatest information bureau in the world? A "Standard Oil" agent is in every hamlet in the country.

■ ■ ■ ■ ■

To show that the coming Techno-Feudal Socialistic New Age New World Order was predicted many years ago, including free trade (today's World Trade Organization) as a vehicle toward it, note the following from the 1907 book, *Lord of the World*, by Robert Hugh Benson (who wrote in it about "the Volor," a fast silent aircraft that could hover):

> In 1917 . . . Communism really began. . . . The new order began then. . . . [After 1989] the final scheme of Western Free Trade. . . . Esotericism is making enormous strides—and that means Pantheism. . . . Humanitarianism is becoming an actual religion itself. It is Pantheism. . . . Patriotism has been dying fast. . . . [There is] this European parliament. . . . [They believe] cooperation is the one hope of the world. . . . [There will be] the alliance of Psychology and Materialism. . . . With the Release Act in 1998 . . . [there were] the ministers of euthanasia. . . . Julian Felsenburgh [Lord of the World] had a magnetic character . . . rising out of the heaving dun-coloured waters of American Socialism like a vision. . . . Felsenburgh's running the whole thing now. . . . It will mean free trade all over the world. . . . [His] speech consisted off a brief announcement of the great fact of Universal Brotherhood. . . . The new era has begun. . . . Party must unite with party, country with country, and continent with continent. . . . Felsenburgh was called the Son of Man . . . the Savior of the World. . . . Persecution was com-

> ing. . . . It involved all the stupendous force of Socialism directed by a brilliant individual. . . . America was powerless: the balance of the world was overwhelmingly against her. . . . This appearance of peace has deceived many. . . . The press was engineered with extraordinary adroitness. . . . The world is one now, not many. Individualism is dead. It died when Felsenburgh became President of the World. . . . For any one to say that they believe in God—it is high treason. . . . The Humanity Religion was the only one. Man was God. . . . No actual point of light breaking the appalling vault of gloom.

The Holy Bible informs us in Ephesians 6:12 that we wrestle "against principalities, against powers, against the rulers of the darkness of this world, against spiritual wickedness in high places." We are further told in Second Corinthians 4:4 that "the god of this world hath blinded the minds of them which believe not, lest the light of the glorious gospel of Christ, who is the image of God, should shine unto them." But John 16:11 says that "the prince of this world is judged," and First Corinthians 7:23 informs and admonishes us that we "are bought with a price; be not ye the servants of men."

▪ ▪ ▪ ▪ ▪

The New York Times, March 27, 1922, prints New York City mayor John Hylan's speech stating:

> The real menace of our republic is this invisible government which like a giant octopus sprawls its slimy length over city, state and nation. Like the octopus of real life, it operates under cover of a self-created screen. It seizes in its long and powerful tentacles our executive officers, our legislative bodies, our schools, our courts, our newspapers, and every agency created for the public protection. It squirms in the jaws of darkness and thus is the better able to clutch the reins of government, secure enactment of the legislation favorable to corrupt business, violate the law of impunity, smother the press and reach into the courts. To depart from mere generalizations, let me say at the head of this octopus are the Rockefeller–Standard Oil interests and a small group of powerful banking houses generally referred to as the international bankers. The little coterie of powerful international bankers virtually run the United States government for their own selfish purposes. They practically control both political parties, write political platforms, make catspaws of party leaders, use the leading men in private organizations, and resort to every device to place in nomination for high public office only such candidates as will be amendable to the dictates of corrupt big business. They connive at centralization of government on the theory that a small group of hand-

picked, privately controlled individuals in power can be more easily handled than a larger group among whom there will most likely be men sincerely interested in public welfare. These international bankers and Rockefeller–Standard Oil interests control the majority of newspapers and magazines in this country. They use the columns of these papers to club into submission or drive out of office public officials who refuse to do the bidding of the powerful corrupt cliques which compose the invisible government.

Author's Notes

1. Less than two years before Prof. Carroll Quigley's death, *The Washington Post* printed an article about him (Quigley) titled, "The Professor Who Knew Too Much." George Orwell died the year after his *1984* was published. And President Lincoln was assassinated less than five months after he wrote to William Elkin on November 21, 1864:

   "I see in the near future a crisis approaching that unnerves me and causes me to tremble for the safety of my country. As a result of the war, corporations have been enthroned and an era of corruption in high places will follow, and the money power of the country will endeavor to prolong its reign by working upon the prejudices of the people until all wealth is aggregated in a few hands, and the Republic is destroyed. I feel at this moment more anxiety for the safety of my country than ever before, even in the midst of war."

   In the famous Fabian H. G. Wells' *Anticipations of the Reaction of Mechanical and Scientific Progress Upon Human Life and Thought* (1901), there is a chapter titled "The Larger Synthesis," in which he declares:

   "In its more developed phases I seem to see the new republic as a sort of outspoken secret society, with which even the prominent men of the ostensible state may be openly affiliated. . . . The new republicans will constitute an informal and open freemasonry. In all sorts of ways they will be influencing and controlling the apparatus of the ostensible governments."

   And in his chapter about "The New Republic," he states that

"the ethical system which will dominate the world state, will be shaped primarily to favor . . . beautiful and strong bodies, clear and powerful minds . . . and to check the procreation of base and servile types. . . . The method that must in some cases still be called in to the help of man is death . . . the merciful obliteration of weak and silly and pointless things. The new ethic will hold life to be a privilege and a responsibility, . . . and the alternative in right conduct between living fully, beautifully, and efficiently, will be to die. . . . The men of the new republic will have little pity and less benevolence. . . . The men of the new republic will not be squeamish either in facing or inflicting death. . . . They will have an ideal that will make killing worth the while. . . . The state will be the reserve guardian of all children. If they are being under-nourished, if their education is being neglected, the state will step in, take over the responsibility of their management, and enforce their charge upon the parents. . . . The new republic will aim to establish . . . a world state with a common language and a common rule. All over the world its . . . control will run."

Alfred Milner carried forth with Rhodes' scheme after Rhodes' death, and in the second volume of Frederic Whyte's *The Life of W.T. Stead* (1915), Whyte states that "Milner himself, it seems, had cherished a somewhat similar project for a band of Companions of St. George." This is interesting in that the College of St. George was a key element in the motion picture, *The Brotherhood of the Bell,* about a secret elite considered to be "*The* Establishment" controlling people's lives (the motion picture stars Glenn Ford, William Conrad, and others). A *free* videotape of this motion picture can be obtained from Peter Ford (son of Glenn Ford and a talk-show host) if one orders one hundred dollars of material from him (materials listed on his website, *http://www.peterford.com*).

2. In the Fabians' *New Statesman & Society* (April 9, 1993), *History Today* editor Gordon Marsden wrote:

"The flaws in the project of the original Fabian socialists were deep—no government 'by the people,' no reform of institutions that could have allowed them that participation. . . . It was government for the people, but not by them. The clarion call was to the New Jerusalem, but the assumption was still that a royal priesthood of Fabian administrators would be needed to supervise its construction. . . . Clinton's victory brings with it a new rhetoric that holds out, once again, the possibility of integrating individual aspiration with a communal structure via the enabling power of the state."

3. *The Journal of American History* (1908, no.4) is "dedicated to the United Nations of the World" and includes the "First Draft of a Constitution for the United Nations of the World" by William Osborne McDowell. The constitution provides for legislative, executive, and judicial branches, with the chief executive called the "Peacemaker." Two of the cabinet secretary positions are to be filled by Carnegie Foundation and Carnegie Institute officials and one position by the ranking trustee of the Cecil Rhodes Oxford Educational Endowment Fund. The Constitution also provides that all armies and navies of the world "shall be placed under the control of the United Nations of the World." The *Journal* begins with the words: "'The most fearful war of the century is coming soon. After the war, will come world-peace—the highest development of the race in this cycle.' This is the prediction made a few days ago by a distinguished political economist." World War I began a few years later.
4. On October 14, 1904, the *London Express* published an article by Andrew Carnegie in which he stated:

   "The peaceful union of Canada and America would lead Britain to a serious view of her position, resulting in the conclusion that Cecil Rhodes reaches. . . . Mr. Stead recounts that Mr. Rhodes went to Lord Rothschild and laid that scheme before him, who replied, 'This is all very well, if you can get America to join—if not it amounts to nothing!' This led Mr. Rhodes to a study of the subject, and the result was he saw clearly that Lord Rothschild was right. . . . He saw that it was to the (American) Republic, not to the British settlements his country had to look for the coming reunion of his race, with Britain in her rightful place as parent of all." (See *The Network of Power and Part II The New World Order: Chronology and Commentary* by Dennis Laurence Cuddy and Robert Henry Goldsborough, published by the American Research Foundation.)
5. On November 27, 1915, Columbia University president Nicholas Murray Butler (on the executive committee of the Carnegie Endowment for International Peace) delivered an address, "A New World Order Is Being Born" to the Union League of Philadelphia

in which he stated: "The old world order changed when this war storm broke—the old world order died with the setting of the day's sun and a New World Order is being born while I speak." In *Tragedy and Hope*, Prof. Quigley refers to Butler as "J. P. Morgan's chief spokesman from ivied halls."

6. Ralph W. Page of *The Philadelphia Bulletin* staff wrote in that newspaper on May 5, 1942, an article, "Plan for Federation of World Definitely Under Way in U.S.," specifically referring to the Humber "Declaration" and its success in state government resolutions supporting a Constitution for the Federation of the World. Page wrote: "It is no longer an idea, it is an institution. With this hard-won background and recognition, the scheme now is to tackle Pennsylvania and the larger states."
7. The January 1919 edition of *International Conciliation* (connected with the Carnegie organization) focuses upon "A League of Nations." The American Association for International Conciliation (with executive committee members Nicholas Murray Butler, Stephen Henry Olin, Joseph P. Grace, and Thomas W. Lamont with J. P. Morgan, among others) sends a cover letter with this edition of the journal, and begins the letter with the words: "The peace conference has assembled. It will make the most momentous decisions in history, and upon these decisions will rest the stability of the new world order and the future peace of the world."
8. The word "front" was also used in *The Wise Men* (1986) co-authored by CFR member Walter Isaacson (Rhodes Scholar 1974–76). In the book is quoted the following passage from Arthur Schlesinger, Jr.'s *A Thousand Days* (1965): "The New York financial and legal community was the heart of the American establishment . . . its front organizations, the Rockefeller, Ford and Carnegie foundations and the Council on Foreign Relations." Isaacson's book is about six leaders who "shaped a new world order," were internationalists, and had a "common outlook." One of the six was Chip Bohlen, who was quoted as saying about socialism: "Maybe that is the road we ought to go down."

   Charles E. (Chip) Bohlen was first secretary to the American embassy in Moscow during the Second World War, and he was President Roosevelt's interpreter at the Teheran conference with Stalin. Based upon Bohlen's extensive notes on a private talk between FDR and Stalin there on December 1, 1943, David Lawrence in *The Philadelphia (Evening) Bulletin* (June 19, 1961) wrote:

"Documents just published by the State Department show that a President of the United States went to a 'summit' conference during World War II and made a deal with the Communist dictator—Joseph Stalin—whereby much of Poland's territory was deliberately conceded to Russia and the way was paved for similar deals that permitted the Communists to grab small countries (Lithuania, Latvia, Estonia). What was even worse, a President of the United States told a foreign ruler that his own decisions were related to a fear he might not retain a bloc of votes of American citizens of Polish extraction and that, for this reason, the deal had to be kept secret—at least until a presidential election was over. Actually, these facts have not been disclosed until now."

9. Early in January 1995 *The New York Times* special features sent over its wires an article by CFR president Leslie Gelb (a shortened version of his article in the CFR's November–December 1994 *Foreign Affairs*) in which he wrote: "The very long process of shaping a more effective and responsible United Nations must begin. This will require some sacrifices of sovereignty. . . . Multilateralism . . . is a fact not to be debated, but absorbed into American strategy." And in March 1995 President Clinton nominated CFR member (and Trilateralist) John M. Deutch to be the new head of the CIA.

The Christian Science Monitor (August 8, 1927) quoted from an address to the World Federation of Education Associations (WFEA) by Dr. Augustus Thomas (commissioner of education for Maine) at their Toronto congress:

"If there are those who think we are to jump immediately into a new world order, actuated by complete understanding and brotherly love, they are doomed to disappointment. If we are ever to approach that time, it will be after patient and persistent effort of long duration. The present international situation of mistrust and fear can only be corrected by a formula of equal status, continuously applied, to every phase of international contacts, until the cobwebs of the old order are brushed out of the minds of the people of all lands. This means that the world must await a long process of education and a building up of public conscience and an international morality, or, in other words, until there is a world-wide public sentiment which will back up the modern conception of a world community. This brings us to the international mind, which is nothing more or less than the habit of thinking of foreign relations and business affecting the several countries of the civilized world as free co-operating equals. . . ."

Dr. Thomas and the National Education Association were largely responsible for the formation of the WFEA, founded in 1923 by Paul Monroe.

10. Quigley further states: "The substantive financial powers of the world were in the hands of these investment bankers (also called 'international' or 'merchant' bankers) who remained largely behind the scenes in their own unincorporated private banks. These formed a system of international cooperation and national dominance which was more private, more powerful, and more secret than that of their agents in the central banks. This dominance of investment bankers was based on their control over the flow of credit and investment funds in their own countries and throughout the world. They could dominate the financial and industrial systems of their own countries by their influence over the flow of current funds through bank loans, the discount rate, and the rediscounting of commercial debts; they could dominate governments by their control over current government loans and the play of the international exchanges."
11. In *Tragedy and Hope,* Prof. Quigley said that Bank of England governor Montagu Norman is reported to have said of himself: "I hold the hegemony of the world."
12. Lord Lothian in *The* (London) *Observer,* November 27, 1938, wrote: "But, though few yet realize it, the old anarchy of multitudinous national sovereignties is about to dissolve—and quickly at that. . . . World unity is, of course, at present entirely out of sight. But that the world is going to fall into four or five main political and economic groups, each in great measure self-supporting, each under the leadership of a great State equipped with modern military and air power, at any rate for a time, seems certain. Nothing that we can do can prevent it."
13. In *The Philadelphia Inquirer* (May 2, 1943), reporter Alexander Kendrick wrote that on May 1 in Washington, U.S. Supreme Court Justice Owen Roberts declared that "an international government, with police power over every individual citizen in the nations

belonging to it—instead of over merely the national governments as such—is the only way to keep the peace after this war (World War II). . . . The individual citizen's loyalty and responsibility to the international government would stand over his loyalty to his own country."

14. Just *before* the attack upon Pearl Harbor by the Japanese (December 7, 1941), Maurice Gomberg prepared a map of the world reorganizing nations into regional groups (e.g., the federated "United States of South America," etc.). Included in his "policy" for this "post-war new world" were the following:

"The U.S.S.R. shall acquire control of the liberated, disorganized adjacent areas and those of Germany-Austria to be re-educated and eventually incorporated as equal republics of the U.S.S.R.; a World League of Nationalities with arbitration and supervision powers shall be organized; a World Court with punitive powers of absolute boycott, quarantine, blockade and occupation by international police, against lawbreakers of international morality shall be organized; to reduce the numerical power of the aggressor nations (Axis Powers), as a potential military advantage, a Population Control Policy shall be elaborated and applied in the quarantined areas; in the New World Moral Order which we seek to establish . . . the following fundamental economic changes are imperative—nationalization of all natural resources and equitable distribution of same to all nations, everywhere in the world."

The next year, the Carnegie Endowment for International Peace made available reprints of a *Common Sense Magazine* (April 1942) article by Eugene Staley in which he stated:

"Political boundaries must be made economically permeable. . . . Steps must be taken for effectively limiting the economic sovereignty of states (nations), so that they will not have the power to restrict trade at national frontiers as they choose. . . . It would be desirable to do this through supra-national collaborative agencies. . . . The techniques of gradualism depend for their success on the development of unity under the influence of successive acts of practical collaboration. . . . Political 'machinery' is not merely a means of executing a common will that already exists; it is also a means of *forming* a common will."

In *The Philadelphia Inquirer* (June 18, 1942), reporter William Murphy, Jr. wrote that on June 17, "Undersecretary of State

Sumner Welles called for the early creation of an international organization . . . the setting up of a new world order on a permanent basis."

15. *The Philadelphia Inquirer* (December 7, 1943) published an article by Ely Culbertson, in which he stated: "How are we going to have an effective (international) police force without conflict with national sovereignty? Specifically, a world police force, to be effective, must be stronger than any possible aggressor nation. But how will you persuade the big nations like the United States, the U.S.S.R., or Great Britain . . . to disarm? There is some reason for this reluctance. A powerful world police force under a world government could, conceivably, become tyrannical and abusive. It could become the instrument of a clique which, having a monopoly of weapons, might stop progress among the nations and seek to impose on the whole world the will of a small ruling class."
16. Carlton Kemp Allen (Rhodes Scholar and warden of Rhodes House, 1931–52) wrote in *Forty Years of Rhodes Scholarship* (1944) that "the Rhodes Trustees will not be satisfied until a Rhodes Scholar is President of the United States. . . ."
17. In *The New York Sunday News* (June 18, 1944), Ted Lewis wrote: "Major elements of President Roosevelt's plan for a postwar security organization, it developed today (June 17, Washington, D.C.), are on the model of a 'community of states' blueprint drafted under the auspices of the Carnegie Endowment for International Peace."
18. *The Philadelphia Inquirer* (September 7, 1948) reported that in Rome, Italy, on September 6, U.S. Senator Alben Barkley was elected one of the vice-presidents of the Interparliamentary Union and said:

    "One of the aims of this union is to create a world government. But I must say as a personal opinion that the time is not yet mature for what we mean by world government. We must create a more efficient organization here and we must strengthen the United Nations before we can achieve our goal of world government."
19. Jonathan Kozol (Rhodes Scholar 1958–59) would write *The Night Is Dark And I Am Far From Home* (1975) in which he described as "ideological deception" the "identification of 'the good' with U.S. interests, and 'the bad' with Eastern, Marxist-Leninist direction."

And he described students' pledge of allegiance to the American flag as "participation in a ritual of unforgivable deceit."

20. The *Chicago Tribune* (April 25, 1949) published "Globalists Run United States, Says Senator Malone—Blood and Money Ties Bared" by Walter Trohan, who wrote:

    "Over cocktails at a recent Washington dinner party, Supreme Court Justice Felix Frankfurter was asked by a German Rhodes scholar who really runs the United States. Sipping on his second old-fashioned, the Vienna-born jurist, who has been acknowledged as the outstanding power behind the New Deal throne for sixteen years, smiled knowingly and answered sententiously: 'The real rulers of a nation are undiscoverable.'"
21. *The Times-Herald* (Washington, D.C.) on October 11, 1943, published, "Rhodes Scholars Find Havens in New Deal Press, Radio," in which was stated: "Not one of the Anglophile Oxonians is employed on a newspaper fighting for the preservation of the Republic against the widespread conspiracy of the internationalists and New Dealers."
22. Richard Lugar will become a U.S. senator in 1977 and later vote for NAFTA and GATT. He will also support the objectionable U.N. Convention on the Rights of the Child, which will be signed by U.S. Ambassador to the United Nations Madeleine Albright, on February 16, 1995, for the Clinton administration.
23. The year prior to State Department document 7277, "The Technical Problems of Arms Control" was published in 1960. It was sponsored by the Institute for International Order and authored by, among others, Arthur Larson (Rhodes Scholar 1932–35) who was director of the World Rule of Law Center. Larson would also be a speaker at "Dilemma 66" at Southwestern at Memphis in 1966 where John David Alexander, Jr. (Rhodes Scholar 1954–57) was president (1965–69). In 1968 it was announced that Saul Alinsky (who was admired by Hillary Rodham), who had criticized "narrow nationalism" in *Reveille for Radicals*, and who would have an Acknowledgment to Lucifer in the front of *Rules for Radicals*, would be a speaker at "Dilemma 69" the next year. When Alexander was criticized in a letter for allowing Alinsky to be invited, he responded: "Free speech." Though Alinsky ultimately did not speak there for some reason, Senator George McGovern did. In 1981 Alexander became American secretary of the Rhodes

Scholarship Trust. In 1998, Elliot Gerson will become American secretary of the Rhodes Scholarship Trust.

24. Bill Clinton would later say concerning Senator Fulbright: "He had a real impact on my desire to become a citizen of the world." (See David Maraniss' article, "Bill Clinton and Realpolitik U.: In '68 Five Georgetown Students Shared a House With a View of the World," in *The Washington Post,* October 25, 1992.)

25. *The Philadelphia (Evening) Bulletin* (April 30, 1971) published, "Nationalism Said to Hinder World Order" by William Nazzaro, in which he quotes Bryn Mawr College president Harris L. Wofford, Jr., as saying on April 29:

    "Is there any greater anachronism than the so-called sovereign nation-state, parading around a little planet, armed with atomic weapons, missiles and old-fashioned bombers, claiming the right to conscript soldiers and make war at will? Its pretensions need to be punctured, its overblown powers need to be deflated. Like J. Edgar Hoover, the absolutely sovereign nation-state has stayed too long." Wofford will become a U.S. Senator from Pennsylvania in 1991.

26. Gardner continued to explain how GATT was part of the plan, in the following words:

    "The hopeful aspect of the present situation is that even as nations resist appeals for 'world government' and 'the surrender of sovereignty,' technological, economic and political interests are forcing them to establish more and more far-reaching arrangements to manage their mutual interdependence. . . . Among other things, we will be seeking new rules in the GATT to cover a whole range of hitherto unregulated nontariff barriers. These will subject countries to an unprecedented degree of international surveillance over up to now sacrosanct 'domestic' policies. . . . GATT arrangements for consultation, conciliation and enforcement of its decisions will have to be greatly improved. . . . Despite the constitutional impasse over *U.N. peacekeeping,* there will in practice be increasing resort to U.N. forces to contain local conflicts. . . . New GATT procedures should be created requiring advance notice, consultation, authoritative interpretation of rules, and settlement of disputes by impartial conciliation commissions under GATT auspices. . . . Multilateral sanctions may even have to be applied to countries that are not GATT members."

This last statement will be worth remembering regarding GATT and WTO proponents' claim that the U.S. can simply withdraw from them if things don't go our way. Gardner continued:

"Unilateral U.S. action will look to others as a destructive act of nationalism unless it is related to multilateral rules and procedures. . . . Some mutually agreed limitations of sovereignty are essential to give full possibilities to the sovereignty of all. . . . We will need to find better ways of enforcing the rules, as by multilateral action that denies benefits and applies punishments. . . . We might begin, very gradually, to deflect the divisive tendencies of nationalism that are now emerging and to exploit the latent possibilities for strengthening the international system."

Gardner would also be a member of the Carnegie Endowment for International Peace National Commission on America and the New World, and he is still on the editorial advisory board of the American Movement for World Government located at 777 U.N. Plaza in New York City.

27. In the *Congressional Record* (February 27, 1958, pp. 3004–5), Senator Malone also stated:

"I am happy that the American people could observe the coalition pushing the world distribution of American jobs and importing unemployment through free trade, or free imports. . . . The International Trade Organization, which was proposed when Mr. Acheson was Secretary of State, was part of the great plan to transfer distribution of American markets to Geneva. The ITO was rejected when it came before Congress, so the international free traders have brought forward the same scheme in the same package but under a different label. . . . Secretary of State Dulles testified before the Senate Finance Committee in 1955, under my questioning, that: 'The President may, at his discretion, sacrifice a part or all of any American industry, if he believes that his foreign policy would be furthered thereby.' This is possible under the 1934 Trade Agreements Act as extended to June of this year. . . . In 1947, President Truman transferred the constitutional responsibility of Congress to regulate foreign trade through the adjustment of the duties on tariffs to Geneva, Switzerland, under the operation called GATT, the General Agreement on Tariffs and Trade. All of this was done under the 1934 Trade Agreements Act, as extended."

28. McCloy was also assistant to Secretary of War Henry Stimson and primarily responsible for the firings of Generals George Patton and Douglas MacArthur. Furthermore, McCloy was architect of the Marshall Plan, president of the World Bank, and chairman of the Ford Foundation, CFR chairman (1953–70), largely responsible for the U.S. government's agreement not to overthrow Fidel Castro after 1962, on the Warren Commission investigating the assassination of President Kennedy, behind the creation of OPEC, and honorary trustee of the Aspen Institute for Humanistic Studies.
29. One way that the global rulers could keep track of everyone would be microchip implants in people. In that regard, *The Los Angeles Times* (August 17, 1994, p. D5) printed an article by Kathleen Wiegner describing the "SmartDevice," a microchip with relevant information "already in about 100 LipoMatrix breast implants tested since October on women in Britain, Italy and Germany. . . . SmartDevice, the chip, which is about the size of a grain of rice, is manufactured by Hughes Identification Devices, a subsidiary of Hughes Aircraft Co. . . . (One) could retrieve the information from the chip using a 'gun' that emits a radio beam. The gun operates in much the same way that decoders in supermarkets decipher bar coding. The information on the chip would also be recorded on a computer-linked global registry."
30. Pertaining to those "who would rule over us," one might refer to (a) Philip Freneau's article in *American Museum* (July 1792) concerning how the power elite might attempt to take over the U.S. in the future; (b) David Korten's *When Corporations Rule the World* (1995); (c) *Vanity Fair* (November 1997) which has on its cover "The 65 Leaders Who Shape and Rule the World Today: A Portrait of World Power."